At the Edge of the Village

AT THE EDGE
OF THE VILLAGE:
Musings of a Missionary Wife

Lisa
Leidenfrost

CANON PRESS   *MOSCOW, IDAHO*

Lisa Leidenfrost, *At the Edge of the Village: Musings of a Missionary Wife*

© 2004 by Lisa Leidenfrost
Published by Canon Press, P.O. Box 8729, Moscow, ID 83843
800-488-2034 / www.canonpress.org

04 05 06 07 08 09   9 8 7 6 5 4 3 2 1

Printed in the United States of America.

Illustrations by:
Abigail Gutting pages 14, 66, 124 and 158 and
Noai Leidenfrost pages 48, 90, and 164.

Cover design by Paige Atwood.

Library of Congress Cataloging-in-Publication Data

Leidenfrost, Lisa.
   At the edge of the village : musings of a missionary wife / Lisa Leidenfrost ; illustrated by Abigail Gutting and Noai Leidenfrost.
      p. cm.
   Contents: Background — Africa orientation course — Choosing a house site — Our home — Language learning — Culture know — Culture shock — Part II: family life — Squirming in Africa — The pig dig — The eclipse — Hunting — Mice — The secret garden — Noai — Civilizations — A typical day — A tropical storm — Part III: village life — Alexis's wedding — Christmas — Handling disputes the Bakw way — Cultural event — Translation — A memorable review session — Part IV: animals — Mongooses and the pond — Barnyard chatter — Goose knots — Flying hen — Snake hunt — Stinker — Choir of clucking hens — Elusive crocodile (by Noai) — Chicken obstacle course — Wild things — Part V: people — Javier and the eggplant field — The old Harrist priest and the locked book — A sketch on death — Josephine — Part VI: culture — The magic trick — Mother-in-law — Hospitality — Plump ladies — Smith's ghost — Revenge of the market ladies — A trip to town — A visit from the states — Part VIII: trials — Thorns and roses — Opening the floodgates — Typhoid — Letter to a missionary friend — Out of sync (trials of a peculiar nature) — Goodbyes — Entering the door — Part VIII: school — Unusual art — Obstacle course — The guineas and their mama — God is good.
   ISBN 1-59128-017-6 (pbk.)
   1. Missionaries—Africa—Biography. 2. Missionaries—United States—Biography. I. Gutting, Abigail. II. Leidenfrost, Noai. III. Title.
   BV3500.L45 2004
   266'.00967—dc22
                                  2003026787

Contents

Acknowledgments

Thanks to my good friend Bev, who is currently the only one of my stateside friends to have entered my world in Africa. She is the wife of the famed 'Tutu' (you will read about him later). She was one of the sparks that ignited the fire that became this book. Most importantly, she believed in me when I had ceased to believe in myself.

Thanks to my two top reviewers, David Kohl and Philip Saunders. Who (quite frustratingly) wouldn't let anything slip by. A big thanks to the rest of my team of reviewers, commentators, encouragers and grammar helpers who did quite a bit behind the scenes.

Thanks to Susan Gutting who is my daughter's art teacher. She is also the mother of my other illustrator, Abby. I must confess I have never seen anyone take so much raw material as she has had in her students, and bring out their hidden talent to enable them to create something truly beautiful.

A special thanks to my children who have provided ample subjects for my stories. These are stories that I hope will be passed down through the generations in our line, and join a stream of accumulated stories for God's glory, the end of which is the culmination of 'His story' at the end of all time.

Last but not least, thanks to my husband who considers this book just as much his as it is mine with the only difference in that I did the initial writing. He is the one with the knowledge for the cultural writings and did some ghost writing for me on occasion. He is the initiator and overseer of the Bakwe project as well as leader of our family. I am just the recorder of events.

As Jeremiah Burroughs said, every comfort you have is a forerunner of those eternal mercies you shall have with God in Heaven, Not only are the consolations of God's Spirit the forerunners of those eternal comforts you shall have in Heaven, but when you sit at your table, and rejoice with your wife and children and friends, you may look upon every one of those as a forerunner, yea the very earnest penny of eternal life to you.

Preface

Step into our world, a place of laughter and tears, trials and hopes, events captured and stories told. They are stories of life, lived out on the mission field in Africa where the hand of God is ever present in every situation.

They are stories of daily events, of cultural experiences recounted, of friends loved and lost, and of trials surmounted.

They are stories of bothersome situations turned to laughter as God gives us the ability to find humor in various hardships—a humor that has kept us sane over all these years.

They are mostly stories of the familiar things in life, the little things that lend spice to our daily experience. Not all of missionary life is extraordinary or bizarre. Most of it is just normal, common events that unfold one day into another. And because God is good, there is a beauty in living, a purpose beyond our own mere existence that can make even the smallest things we do burst with life and meaning, laughter and delight. Too often these small, commonplace things go unnoticed unless they are caught and brought to life in words, words which become a lens that can, even if for a single moment, bring this ever-present beauty into focus.

Part I
Background

1
Africa Orientation Course

We stepped outside to look around. Csaba (*chawba*) shone his flashlight down on the ground. There was no ground; only a black mass moving toward us. I stood there stupefied, looking at an endlessly flowing stream of ants. We went into the kitchen. On the walls were rivers of surging ants, up the walls, down the walls, on the floor and into the pots and pans, in a seamless black carpet. I could hear them make threatening, crackling noises as if they were soldiers out for booty and we were the victims. I had heard about these ants but had never actually experienced them until that night. It was said that they could kill and consume a bound animal, no matter how large, leaving only the bones in their wake. I shivered and went back to our two young children, who were sleeping on the couch, while Csaba put some kerosene and water in a bucket to ward off the army. I was left alone on the couch, afraid to go back to the bedroom where the driver ant raid had first begun. If we were experiencing only the orientation to Africa now, I wondered what the real thing would be like when we started our project in a village.

Our first African experience together as a family of four was the African Orientation Course held in Cameroon, before we were to head to Ivory Coast where we planned to start a translation project among the Bakwé people. We were excited about this new phase of our lives, but when reality set in during our orientation, we finally realized how difficult our situation might be, and just how much we would need God's grace in the future.

In the first part of our orientation, we were to live with other would-be missionaries in dorm-like rooms for about five weeks, learning how to live with each other and our new culture. We would receive training on health, medicine, African culture, village living, and crisis management during times of political upheaval. This was all fine and good; little happened to ruffle us—except for the medical lectures. I don't think most of the missionaries had realized what a dangerous place Africa could be, and many had brought their young families with them. At the time, we had a two-year-old son (Hans) and a three-month-old daughter (Noai). I remember sitting in on a medical lecture with my baby daughter in my lap along with rows of other missionaries. We were all diligently taking notes as the nurse talked about the different diseases we might run into and how to treat them.

As she went on and on about malaria, schistosomiasis, sleeping sickness, and the various dangers we could possibly face from either the diseases or the medications to treat them, she became acutely aware that the room was silent and that note-taking had almost stopped. Most eyes were glued to her in abject horror, except for a few impassive males who were by nature not affected by much to begin with. She looked around the room, sighed, and then said, "Okay, let's stop the lecture and sing 'Turn Your Eyes upon Jesus.'"

That was Phase One. Phase Two would test our real resolve to be missionaries in Africa. In the "village living phase" we would be dropped off family by family to live in the home of a real African family for five weeks. Those who could, would work on a community project to help the village during part of the day. Our living conditions varied from mud and stick houses with holes in the walls and little privacy to cement floors, solid walls, and tin roofs.

We actually got a nice situation in a house with a concrete floor, solid walls, and no live-in family since the owner was happily elsewhere. Concrete floors were especially appreciated because at the age of four months, my baby daughter began to crawl. (What was she doing? I didn't want her to crawl yet!) Concrete floors may seem uncomfortable for crawling purposes, but after the medical lectures I now knew what she could catch from being in constant contact with the bare soil.

Others may have had different experiences, but we actually found the village living phase much to our liking, except for a few minor details—

such as no toilet and no running water. To get running water, Csaba and I had to put the children on our backs and walk to a stream. It took us half an hour to make one round trip with four meager buckets of water. We learned how to conserve water and never to take it for granted. A full bath could be taken in half a bucket; washing dishes took less. The problem was washing diapers and clothes by hand, which was solved only by packing the children on our backs and hiking down to the stream again. The hardest part was trying to keep my energetic, now-crawling baby daughter within the confines of the muddy bank, and our inquisitive young son from exploring the bushes alone while we washed our things by hand near the stream; we had sat in on snake lectures as well as medical lectures.

Snakes were to be the least of our problems; though we imagined several, we never saw one. What we did see constantly were the small creatures that hid in the dark crevices under our bed, and the millions of assorted black specks that came to raid the house at night. Since the children were so young and we were still in uncharted waters, we set up little beds attached to our big one and draped the large mosquito net over us all. We failed to realize that more was needed than just draping the net over the bed and letting it fall to the floor. One must also tuck the net under the mattress so that nothing that has been hiding under the bed all day can crawl up in the bed at night.

I acutely remember waking up in the middle of the night to see a big, fat, hairy spider hanging on the inside of the net just inches above my nose, hideous in appearance and horrible in size. I decided to awaken my sleeping husband to get rid of it since my own intense fear of spiders prevented any other action on my part. It is his duty anyway, written in some unspoken job description for husbands that dates back to the beginning of time. Between us there has never been any dispute—spiders and such are his job. Waking him up wasn't easy, but eventually he was coherent enough to realize my distress. After this, all was well until the driver ants appeared.

Driver ants really are a wonder of the African forest. They are one of God's marvels and I know that I should appreciate them more, but somehow at the time I couldn't. Drivers are nomadic ants of the tropical rain forest that invade an area *en masse* and wipe it clean of anything even vaguely edible. When they come in, they simply take over. They can kill an immobilized animal of any size due to their sheer numbers. When they are disturbed, they bite with such force that you can actually pull the body of the ant off and leave the head with its huge pinchers still intact in your clothing or skin. You need to crush the head to get them off. Some people use them as sutures for wounds, making the ant bite the two sides of the cut together, then pulling off the body. Apparently it works very well (we haven't tried it).

Since our house was on the edge of the forest, the driver army decided to drop in for a casual call one night after our net was securely tucked in and quite thankfully spiderless. It did not remain antless. I don't know how they did it, but the determined ants somehow got under the net. I woke to hear my two-year-old son starting to cry. I reached over to pat him on the back and I drew back my hand with a cry of pain and surprise. Something had bit me hard. I groped for the flashlight and woke Csaba. Drivers! They had come up the net and into our bed. I grabbed our two sleepy kids and sat them on my lap away from any more approaching ants. Csaba in the mean time surveyed the situation with his flashlight. There were only a few drivers in the net now, but many would soon follow. It is very difficult to stay the advance of a determined troop. Csaba told me we would have to leave the bedroom until the raid was over.

Csaba took the flashlight and shone it on the bedroom floor, revealing the rivers of ants that were flowing by the bed and into the hall. Since the ants proceed by following another ant directly in front of them, and thus leave bare patches of floor untouched between their ranks, Csaba took our sleepy son and led me, with our daughter in my arms, from island to island of floor through the rivers of ants. As long as you don't step in their immediate path they don't seem to know that you are there. We made it to the living room, set our children on the couch, and patted them back to sleep. We then went to investigate the path of the army.

It was then that Csaba went out to splash the kerosene-water on the ants to make them retreat. When one ant recognizes that a foul substance has appeared in his path, he will pass the message on and the whole troop will flank out in a different direction. They are frighteningly organized. If your placement of kerosene water is strategic enough you can get the whole army to move on to better ground. Csaba spent the next hour coaxing the drivers away from the house. After the ants had retreated from the bedroom, I settled the kids back into their beds. We would repeat this little routine two more times in the next five weeks.

If the Village Phase didn't "make men" out of us, the Forest Phase certainly would. In this part of the orientation we were to hike deep into the rain forest and be dropped off family by family into different parts of the forest, within earshot of each other but out of sight. We would then put up a shelter and spend the night. The leaders would camp in a central location and come to the aid of anyone who needed it. The women with their babies and young children would be allowed to leave the next day; the rest would have to stay an extra two nights. (I must mention that this "Forest Phase" is no longer one of the requirements of the orientation course.)

The one catch was that we were not allowed to take in what we could not carry. After being loaded down with two young kids and all the diapers needed, plus a small baby bed, we didn't have room for much else. We were given some water, but not enough, and a plastic zipper bag full of oatmeal with powdered milk and sugar. This was actually the ration for the children. We guessed that we were somehow supposed to find our food on the forest floor.

After we were dropped off in our spot, Csaba immediately set to work with his machete to build a shelter large enough for the whole family before nightfall. I was of little help since I had to keep my dynamo crawling daughter (why did she have to start crawling?) from leaving the premises and my inquisitive two-year-old son happy. We explored a little and he enjoyed the forest while Daddy was wildly chopping material for our shelter. Hans even grabbed a stick and whacked a few bushes—just like Daddy. He was happy until he got into some stinging ants and started to howl. These small ants actually have poison in their stings that make them feels like bee stings. I calmed him down as best I could with oatmeal and powdered milk.

As I was occupying myself with the kids, my friend came storming down into our camp rather irritated. She brought with her their young daughter. She asked to stay with us for a while until she cooled down. I asked her what had happened and she just said that she and her husband had had a bit of a disagreement over their shelter, one of those little marital spats that one gets into under trying conditions. Maybe they disagreed over where to put the study and the parlor in their little stick shelter. I didn't ask. I told her she was welcomed to stay but ot watch out for the stinging ants. She stayed as long as she needed and left more calmly.

As night approached, the shelter was almost done; Csaba was covered in sweat but pleased with his work. It was a grand A-frame shelter with a platform floor raised off the ground to keep any invading driver ants, unwanted snakes, or spiders from crawling up in our bed at night. This was necessary because we weren't allowed the comfort and security of a mosquito net. Csaba had worked so hard in the heat that we had already run out of our meager supply of drinking water, and he wanted to go into the forest to a stream to get more before darkness set in. We would then boil it to make it safe to drink. As the sun was setting over the forest canopy, the air became damp and the shadows settled in the cracks and crevices of the forest like a thick fog. I knew how fast night came on at the equator. Dusk can last only fifteen minutes before you are plunged into darkness. As the sun disappeared behind the last giant treetop I watched my husband disappear into the forest with his flashlight. I settled down on the shelter with my son and nursing daughter feeling very much alone. We were out of sight of all human habitation. Night had fallen quickly. It seemed like an eternity until I saw a light come bobbing back through the underbrush. Csaba was back and all was now right with the world.

My daughter nursed herself to sleep and lay in her little padded bed. My son was in his pajamas and ready for bed, having already had his supper of dried oatmeal and powdered milk. I had shared in it too as I was hungry and no dinner had come forth from the forest floor. Then my son started to howl. He had come to the conclusion that he wasn't a "man" yet. He had hit his limit and was expressing it in the only way he knew how. I really could not blame him. He'd had no nap, no bath, no normal bedtime routine, was still smarting a bit from the fire ants, had only oatmeal for dinner, a towel for a pillow and sticks for a bed which were not at all to his liking, and to top it off, he was in a *jungle*, of all places! This simply could not to be tolerated.

We comforted him and sang him to sleep, put him down on his bed of towels and sticks, and whispered good-night. Then we were on our own, my husband and I, under a sky brilliantly lit with stars above the upper forest canopy that covered us like the vaulted ceiling of a cathedral. I had always liked camping, and now, once the kids were down, the shelter up, and my husband within reach, I was once again enjoying myself. We had a crackling fire, hot water to sip on (tea was not allowed) and the warm tropical night with all its strange noises to make us feel both eerie and cozy together.

But I believe the most amazing part of that tropical night was the ground itself. We began to notice it was glowing with thousands of tiny specks. It was the most unusual thing I had ever seen. When I bent down and touched one, I found it was a small piece of glowing humus in the dirt. We had no idea why it glowed but it enchanted us—we seemed to be in a magical world with sparkling diamonds above us and glowing fireworks underneath.

After awhile I went to retire on the stick platform with the kids. It was a great master bedroom, parlor, living room, kitchen, study and sitting room all wrapped up into one stick structure. I was proud of my husband. I was proud of his house, and I wondered how my friend was getting on up there in the forest out of sight (but within earshot). As I settled in, Csaba said he didn't feel much like sleeping and would stay up a long time, keeping the fire going—all night, if he needed to. He was good to his word. As for me, *I* slept.

We only found out later what had happened in some of the other camps. When our son let out his 'I've had it' cry, the other wives were huddling on their platforms looking out into that deep dark forest and wondering what wild animals were at that moment devouring the Leidenfrosts. We were all aware what kinds of wild things could stalk those dark depths and a scream was not a reassuring sound. The other wives were very glad to see me at the bus the next morning and to be reassured that we had not been eaten after all.

The wives among us were lucky—we had our husbands to protect and comfort us. But in our group we also had some single women going through the training. We later learned they had adventures too, and not all positive. I doubt that any had ever had much experience with machetes or making shelters before this, but they had to make an effort fast or they would be stuck on the forest floor for the night. This little bit of knowledge was quite enough to spur them on to great efforts to put up a shelter—*any* type of shelter—before nightfall. One woman somehow managed to erect her shelter before dark and settled down on her platform to listen to all the imaginary wild animals (one of them being my son) out in the darkness. As she was contemplating all the things that could be out there, and the fact that she was feeling very much alone, her shelter fell down. This might not have been so bad in and of itself, but the driver ants then decided to pick her camp for one of their nightly raids. Not wanting to share her fallen bed with the army, she had to leave the premises and stand away in the forest somewhere until they left, which was not for quite some time. I don't know if she got much sleep that night, but I do know that she was with us in line for the bus the next morning.

As we sat waiting for the bus with our tired and cranky children, none of the mothers chided the single ladies who were supposed to stay in the forest another night. No one blamed them or even made a cutting remark. When a determined and frustrated single woman has just spent the night in the jungle alone with a bunch of driver ants and wild imaginary animals, without a husband to fend them off, we felt she was entitled to buck the rules.

This training camp was only the beginning of many adventures for all of us. Those who completed it went on to various stations, some to the city to do administration work, some to workshop centers as managers, and some to do teaching. The rest of us—the translators—went on to our own stations, often in very primitive conditions, where our adventures of sickness, wild creatures, political unrest, and village life with its problems and joys were just about to begin. But for now, we were broken in.

What many of us learned during this time was vital for our future survival. We learned our limits, we learned our weaknesses and strengths, but most importantly we learned that we were not very strong in ourselves alone. At times we were fed up, frustrated, or scared, but we learned more and more how to lean on the all-powerful hands of our Father, who would never fail us in all that was yet to come. We did not yet know how many times we would need Him in the future.

2

Choosing a House Site

When we finally arrived in Ivory Coast, we met the team of missionaries that comprised the Ivory Coast branch of Wycliffe. We got along very well with them and spent the next eight months working at the administrative center in the capital city of Abidjan. Then we were sent upcountry to investigate the Bakwé area. We went to stay with another missionary family so Csaba could go into Bakwé territory with the husband to see if a translation was needed and wanted. They set off the next day and after visiting many villages, they knew that a translation was needed and wanted by the people, and they determined which village would be the best one for us to settle in.

After this survey trip, we went back to the city for a short period of time to make some necessary preparations, and then we packed up our things and took off towards our new home: a missionary's house that Csaba had arranged for us to live in while the owners were gone for a year. It was situated on the fringe of Bakwé territory and would allow Csaba to travel to the village each day to build our house. But before he could begin building, he had to procure land for the house. This would not be easy.

When he went to the village with his request for a piece of land, the chief told him there was no *palaver* (argument) over house sites. Csaba could choose any house site available and take it. The chief then took him on a tour, on one side of the village only, showing him all the available sites. Csaba did not really like any, but noticed a very nice site on the other side of the village, situated among some trees, where the chief had not taken him. He mentioned it to the chief, who said again Csaba could have any site he wanted, but were there not some fine sites he had already been shown?

After Csaba came home he described the different locations and we talked about them. I agreed with him that the one by the trees was the only good one. Csaba returned to the village and again he was shown the same sites on the same side of the village. With the knowledge that he could have any site he wished, he told the chief that he wanted the piece of land under the trees he had mentioned before. The chief said he understood, and Csaba could truly have any he wanted since they don't make *palaver* over land sites here. Csaba was to come back the next day to finalize it. Csaba left the village and returned the next day as scheduled with a Christian Baoulé friend named Fulbert.

When they arrived at the chief's courtyard, they noticed there was already a large meeting going on under the outdoor porch. The porch was filled with men who did not look very happy. After greeting everyone, Csaba and Fulbert sat off to the side on a wooden bench, all but ignored. As they looked on at the proceedings, they could see that the meeting area was divided up into two groups, the men on each side yelling at those opposite them.

Csaba leaned over and whispered to Fulbert, "Something really big is happening here. I wonder what they're talking about?" Fulbert didn't know since he couldn't understand Bakwé, so they both sat back and watched. What they saw was interesting. One by one, men got up and aired their grievances, but each time someone talked, another would interrupt him with an angry tone. There was murmuring and grumbling around the group as the factious arguing went on and on. Finally the chief stood up, said something important, and then sat down. After this, many men shot up and started yelling at each other all at once from both sides, and the whole place erupted into tumultuous confusion. As the argument finally died down a little, some men from one side stormed away in a huff. They were followed by more from the same side, all going in the same direction across the road that ran down the middle of the village, until none of them were left. Fulbert leaned over to Csaba and said, "I think they're talking about you. Don't insist on the spot that you wanted. Something's going on here. Take the site that they give you."

After the men left and the commotion settled down, the chief turned to Csaba and said, "We don't make *palaver* over land, and you can have any site you choose, but I suggest that you take the site on the edge of the village across from the soccer field. Csaba agreed to this and sat down to eat with the men. Since he was sitting by a young man who looked friendly, he asked him what the argument had been about. Csaba found out the village was actually made up of two villages, put together by the government to share a single school. The road that ran through the middle of the village was the border between the two clans. One village was dominant over the other and this was manifested by what structures were put on which side. On the chief's side was the school; on the other side was only the soccer field. The chief, in constant competition with the subordinate clan, and wanting the newcomer's prestige, had only shown Csaba sites on his side of the village. It was true he could have any site he wanted—as long as it was on the chief's side. Csaba did not know this and had insisted on a site on the other side of the village.

The men from the "other" side jumped in and insisted he be given land on their side. The chief refused. An argument boiled up, allowing both sides to recount a long history of abuses that each had done to the other. Finally the lesser side stormed away in anger, leaving the chief to give land on the edge of the village, which was supposed to be on more neutral ground. But we noticed even on the fringe of the village, it was still on the chief's side. It would take years for us to win the offended side back over to our cause, but eventually we did, by hiring one of their sons, Alexis, to be our main translator. All was then forgiven.

It had been a difficult road but we'd made it. Now that we had our land, we could build our house. Only then could we settle in for the real challenge—the language. But first things first.

3

Our Home

We like our home. It was designed by Csaba, made out of handmade cement blocks, covered with metal roofing, and put up with help from some African workers. It is actually two separate houses situated at right angles to each other, one being the kitchen house and the other being the sleep house—which has everything else in it. The idea of two houses is the Bakwé way. The kitchen is more of a social area and separate from the sleep house, which is traditionally more private. We like it that way too, especially since it keeps most of the mice in the kitchen and not the other house.

It is nothing fancy but I believe we live quite well. The floor is concrete instead of dirt, with interesting patterns of pigment and cracks running throughout. The walls are cinder block covered in a layer of cement and overlaid with whitewash. Our windows are large and screened with huge wooden shutters to keep out the driving rain. The ceiling is only a mat made of local materials resting on wooden beams—used by our resident mice to do laps around the house at night.

In the big house there are three bedrooms with mosquito nets on each bed—a necessity in a malaria-infested area. There is a bathroom divided into two rooms with an intricate system of pipes that carry the rainwater down from the cistern to the sinks and toilet. It works well when the rains are abundant, which they are most of the year. Our sinks are made out of metal basins bought in the market. Csaba chiseled a drain hole into each one and attached a pipe to the bottom that empties into our own septic system.

We have a courtyard between the kitchen and the sleep house with a covered porch that connects the two houses, allowing us to go from one house to the next without being drenched during a tropical rainstorm. On the end of this porch is the cistern, which catches the rainwater from both roofs, made out of cement and sealed with a special paint. In the farthest corner of the porch we have a mud stove that is used to heat up water in huge iron kettles for our baths at night. On this porch lives one permanent resident, our parrot, who has a nasty habit of commenting on just about everything under the sun in a very smug and saucy manner. He also likes the thrill of hanging onto the screen door as the kids go in and out of the kitchen.

As you enter our large kitchen, you see a long cupboard in the middle dividing the room into two equal spaces. This cupboard allows space for Javier, our cook, to function in the kitchen without bumping into me—an arrangement we both like. On the far wall, Csaba made an ant-free wooden cupboard (ants are the constant plague here) by hanging the cupboard with greased wires from the wall. The base of the cupboard has screw heads sticking out at the bottom that rest in cups of oil attached to a brace coming out of the wall. As long as there is oil in the cups, the cupboard is ant-less. The wooden shelves where I keep my pots and pans are open, covered only with a cloth, which keeps the cockroaches down and the mold on the shelves under control. We have a relic of a western stove through which you can see the cement floor if you look hard enough through the holes in the oven. The oven rack hangs at an erratic angle, which causes waves in the cakes, and the burner grates are so rusted from the humidity that they sometimes just fall apart. But the stove, though inconsistent, works fine and we don't complain—it sure beats cooking over an open fire. (Since the time of this writing, the old stove has died and a new relic of equal grace and virtue replaces it.)

Beyond the kitchen, separated by a wall and a large doorway covered with mosquito netting, is the dining area; the netting keeps out the many flies tagging along into the kitchen behind one's back. The dining area has high windows so we will not be stared at by curious passersby during our meals. All in all, it is a good house.

The courtyard has abundant flowers and a cage of deviant mongooses. Beyond the courtyard is the carport, covered in thin wooden shakes, which is the home of "Ol' Fuzz-Face," our dog. He sits in the soft dirt and terrorizes the chickens when he gets half a chance. Beyond this is a mud and stick guesthouse with an office on one end and a guest room on the other. We have recently built another office across the road which the team has happily moved into. The rabbit pens are off to the side of the guesthouse and filled with potential rabbit dinners. The handmade chicken houses, constructed by my sons, lie beyond that. Many happy hours are spent there holding baby chicks, as well as more than a few unhappy hours killing snakes at night. Beyond that is an intricate yard full of trees of every tropical fruit imaginable, flower bushes of every conceivable bright color, Csaba's honey bees (the African killer bee variety)we try to pretend aren't there, fish ponds filled with stubborn fish, and a small mud house built by Hans and filled with the kids' old bicycles.

On a good portion of the property beyond that are my cocoa and coffee forests. Yes, we grow our own coffee, and we even grind it when the mood is upon us. The mood hasn't been upon us now for quite some time since, quite frankly, it is not the best coffee. That or we have not yet perfected the art of roasting it. We grow our own chocolate as well. It makes wonderful, lumpy, chocolate cake. It's the richest, darkest, crudest chocolate I've ever eaten—we know even less about processing it than we do coffee.

Beyond all this is the "back forty" — the wild areas. Past relics of old vegetable gardens dot the clearings with tangled bush, vines and trees. This is where the kids' imaginations soar and fortresses appear out of a gathering of sticks; empires are fashioned out of a series of tunnels through the thick undergrowth, and lime wars are fought on the edge of my rice field.

There are not many places more beautiful to live, grow and raise three boys and a girl.

4
Language Learning

Once the house was completed and we were happily living in it, the next challenge was to learn Bakwé, a difficult tonal language which had never before been put into written form, and to learn it from people who had never taught it to foreigners before. They just could not understand why we failed to get the tone right and why we would ask for a chicken to unlock the door instead of a key. We were a source of unbounded amusement, especially the time when Csaba went around the village greeting people and telling them that he was currently sleeping. From the first years of frustration, being made the brunt of jokes and laughter, to nearly two years later, Csaba slowly learned the language well enough to be mistaken for a Bakwé by a blind lady. Due to my pregnancy and obligations at home I lagged far behind.

Here is an account of my first feeble attempts at language learning with a tutor at home, quoted from my journal:

A memorable language session today. I asked for a phrase to say, "I'm going now." I wrote it down and then went on to ask her some other things. When I went back to review my first phrase I found that she could not remember what phrase she had given me so she gave me another one instead. Confused, I accepted it. The next day, when I tried to review the second phrase with her, she didn't seem to understand what I was saying so I asked her to repeat it to me again. Since she couldn't remember what she had said, she gave me a third phrase that also meant the same thing — "good-bye." I asked her to repeat the phrase she had given me to begin with so that I could practice something and get it right. She just gave me a quizzical look and said, "But this is it."

I responded, "But this is different from any of the phrases you have given me so far."

She shrugged her shoulders and said, "Just use this one now."

It was frustrating. Ways to say "good-bye" disappeared like magic coins in the magician's hand. What was I to do? I now had three ways to say the same thing but I couldn't use any of them because I could never get her to repeat a phrase long enough to practice it. All she did was give me a new phrase to say supposedly the same thing. I was wondering how many more phrases I would get; I was soon to find out.

Sure enough, by the end of the week I had a total of five different ways to say farewell, none of which I had the privilege of practicing more than once. I was thinking of just choosing one and using it on the people in the village. I guess it would not matter what I used since all they did was laugh at me anyhow. I am the village entertainment in their otherwise routine day.

I think she first gave me a phrase that said, "I'll see you later." The next day she probably shortened it to the way they really say it: "See ya." Then the third day she forgot and probably gave me the equivalent "So long." To a foreigner all the above phrases sound very different and could be curses in disguise for all one knows. I was totally dependent on my language teacher since the phrases could not be verified in a book. *We* were writing the book.

Our technique for learning this unwritten language was to ask questions in French to a chosen tutor in the context of different controlled settings, then use what we learned in real life situations in the village. Since we had no textbook to guide us, we made up our own language lessons from the questions we asked our tutors. It sounds much easier than it really is.

Again I quote my frustrations from my journal:

This week I had another memorable language session. It's a wonder I don't just give up. She gave me a phrase that I wrote down. Then to verify what I had written down, I had her say it again. But she changed the last vowel from *o* to *u*. I called her on it and she said that she had not changed anything, but I heard her! Frustrated, I went on to something else. Then to try to catch her, I asked for the original phrase again. Sure enough she switched back on me once more. I wonder what significance that change has? I wonder which vowel I am supposed to use now? I don't know. I think I'll just put it in residue. ["Residue" is the language learner's pile of undecipherable mysteries that one will eventually try to unravel.]

We went visiting the next day. I tried to use my phrases on people, and boy did I cause a commotion. They applauded and giggled and begged for more. When I continued on, they erupted into laughing. You can imagine how this made me feel. Language learning is not for those with a weak self-image.

It is difficult to enter another culture so vastly different from your own. In order to learn the language well we must go out and actually use it. When we use it, we're laughed at. When we're laughed at, we tend to quit using it, and then we don't learn the language. It can be very difficult. Yet we see they are pleased with our efforts. They are not laughing at us out of meanness but out of pleasure. Sometimes this pleasure is difficult for us to take. But it is all a part of the process of being a missionary, a kind of breaking-in process that someday in the future would be completed.

5

Culture Know

Language learning was one challenge, but living with a culture totally different from our own was quite another. We had not only to learn to say things in the right way with the right accent, but we had to learn how to decipher the unspoken language as well. In each culture, the local people know socially how to act via these cues. They know instinctively how to ask for things and also how to give them, how to receive something given and also how to reject it. They know when to stay and when their welcome is worn out. For example, in Africa if you leave your host's house too soon you will offend; in America you can offend if you stay too long. In Africa you can offend if you don't take food offered; in America you can offend if you do, because everyone knows you are supposed to decline it. Not knowing certain social cues puts you at a loss as to how to act or how to interpret the way others act towards you. It's a baffling feeling.

One day in the very beginning of our life in the village I remember telling my cook something really important that he was supposed to remember. As soon as I opened my mouth to talk, his eyes looked at the ground as if he wasn't paying attention. I asked him if he was really listening to me and his eyes shot up, looked me in the eye with dignity and said, "Of course I am." When I proceeded again, his eyes immediately drifted to the ground in seeming disinterest. I tried to lower my head a little to look up at him to make sure he was with me when he diverted his eyes again away from mine. I found out later that a sign of deep respect—a sign that you are all ears and really listening—is to look at the ground, avoiding eye contact. It is a way of saying nothing is distracting my attention, not even your face. This is the exact opposite from our culture.

Culture shock was not all on our side. My cook had to learn we were different and didn't play the social games by the same rules. In fact we were often clueless to these social games, which everyone played and knew the rules to—everyone except, of course, us. One day my cook and his brother were in the kitchen while I was snapping beans we brought back from the city. Beans are not common in Africa; you could call them a delicacy in our tropical corner of the world where everything seems to mold before it ripens. I was enjoying snapping my beans when my cook came over to me and said, "My, what nice beans you have."

I responded, "Yes, they are." I continued to snap them.

The cook said, "They are so firm and without spot."

"Yes."

There was a silence and he didn't leave. He continued on again. "You know beans are excellent in sauce."

"Yes," I responded. "That they are."

This "Ode to a Bean" routine went on for a little while until I began to put two and two together. "What are you trying to say to me? Do you want some beans?"

Rather shocked at my abruptness, he looked away and said, "Um, uh . . . no!"

At this his brother finally broke in, "Can't you see she's not like the others? She doesn't know what you want. Yes, you do want some beans. Why don't you just tell her up front? She's a little slow."

Yes, I was a bit dense. I had forgotten this was an indirect culture where you need to know how to guess and read into others' actions. We were to have a lot of "fun" with that aspect of the culture in the future.

6
Culture Shock

What is culture shock? It is feeling stupid. It is wondering why everyone else is being stupid. It is humbling and perplexing, exciting and comical. What is culture shock? It is fumbling your way through your new culture, trying to understand them and they you.

We, like every missionary, have had our fair share of it, though Csaba less so, since he grew up in Africa with his missionary parents. He was in his element; I was not. For example, I didn't understand why people kept stopping and staring at us wherever we went. Staring is unacceptable in our home culture, no matter how weird someone may be. Why was it acceptable in theirs? Was it because we were beyond weirdness and into the realm of "now *this* deserves a good stare" (which is not a very reassuring feeling)? I also wondered why people would keep asking us for things, constantly—much more than I thought was polite. Csaba said this giving and taking was part of their culture too.

I had a lot to learn, but I was not the only one to go through culture shock. We were also a strange people to them. I was always asking my cook to do things that at first he didn't really understand, like soaking our vegetables in a sterilizing agent or passing our bread through a flame to kill the germs. When we had first come to the village, I asked my cook to clean, meaning to "gut" or "dress," a chicken for me. I must have used the wrong word, because I was a bit surprised to come out later and find a newly killed and plucked chicken getting a full bath in a tub of soapy water. He had not understood why I had made this unusual request but he knew that I was "different," and out of respect he had not pressed the point.

Other missionaries have run into these little cultural misunderstandings too. We heard one story about a missionary who asked his house help to boil up some drinking water and turn the timer on for twenty minutes. I am not sure exactly how he said it, but when the missionary came back he found a timer set for twenty minutes sitting in a pot of boiling water.

Yes, we missionaries are different. I often wonder what they think of us. One of these moments of cultural incredulity at our expense came years later when I was in the kitchen doing Biology with my kids. We caught some frogs and gave them to Javier, our cook, for lunch. He hit them over the head with a machete so that they died instantly. Before he detached the legs, I opened up the chest of one of them to have my kids look inside. Suddenly I stopped and shouted out in alarm, "The heart is still beating! I thought you said this thing was dead!"

Javier replied, "Yes, frogs are strange that way. They're dead when they are not yet dead."

We went on with the lesson until Alexis, our translator, walked into the kitchen and said in a tone of disgust, "What are you doing?"

I looked up at him and responded casually, "I'm doing surgery on a frog for our science project. Want to watch?" He made a face then left; apparently the cause of science was not enough to justify such a bizarre project.

That encounter may not have been so bad by itself had the dolly dress incident not taken place later on that same afternoon. Noai, my young daughter, didn't have many dolls and she needed more guests for her tea party, so she caught a young "teenage" chicken and put a doll dress on it. I helped her to tie a scarf on its head. The chicken looked, in our opinion, very cute, and Noai went off with her new guest to attend the tea party that was waiting in the back yard. It turned out chickens are not too keen on tea parties, or dresses either, and it shot away from Noai like a bullet—dress, scarf and all. Noai tried to find her reluctant guest and bring it back again, but she soon tired of the search, so I was called on the scene to find it. I wondered if it had gone off to the village.

I was on my way there when I happened to run into Alexis, who was on his way back to work after a break. The chicken decided at this time to make its appearance, running by us on its way to the village. As the decked-out poultry ran by in its blue dress and scarf, Alexis looked up at me incredulously. He smiled, shook his head, and looked to me for an explanation. When I couldn't provide a plausible one, he muttered something incomprehensible in Bakwé, again shook his head, and left to go back to work with Csaba. I didn't know what to say to him, or what he thought of me other than that I was definitely something out of the ordinary. That was all right. He had not yet learned the half of it.

Part II
Family Life

7

Squirming in Africa

We work in a place notorious for things that creep, crawl, shuffle, and jump. These unnameables are fine when out of sight, but when they come onto the premises they rarely fail to make us squirm. Once I was sitting on the couch, minding my own business, when I saw a pair of hairy legs poke down through the fiber mats that form our ceiling. It did not require much closer inspection to know that there was a tarantula up there, and to know with equal certainty that I was not going to be the one to kill it. I shrieked out, "Csaba! There's a big hairy tarantula up there! Kill it!" After all, what are husbands for? He dutifully came in and I noticed that he was smiling. Seeing your husband smile when there is a giant hairy tarantula to be killed is a bit disconcerting, but he made a gallant swoop at the tarantula and dislodged it from the mat. This knocked the hideous creature down onto the floor where it then did what I absolutely detest: it started to crawl away across my floor in all its horrible hairiness in slow-lingering goosesteps! I don't want to speak amiss of my husband, but it took him an awfully long time to kill that spider. He kept missing all those easy shots as I cowered on the couch yelling, "Kill it! Kill it!" I suspect my gallant knight was rather enjoying himself.

He was to get his due a short time later. I rarely have the opportunity to actually see him squirm at anything, since not much fazes him, but I found it is possible. One morning while I was still in bed, Csaba got up and began to dress. As he sleepily put on his pants, he suddenly started dancing wildly in place. I was not sure what gave him the urge to do this violent, early-morning jig, but it was made clear to me a few seconds later when a very fat mouse ran out from the bottom of his pant leg. Csaba carefully removed his pants and made a diligent search through the pockets for the rest of the family, which thankfully had not yet arrived. Ever since then, he's made it one of his early morning routines to shake out his pants and search the pockets.

A rat took up residence in our house. I hate rats almost as much as spiders. We had been after this one for quite some time, but the traps we set out for him had no effect. Finally one night our chance came when he made a fatal mistake— he was sighted in the living room, which had only one escape route. Seizing the opportunity, Csaba blocked the exit and we set to work. With Csaba directing, we set up a funnel system to trap it. His idea was that I would guard the barrier while he chased the rat into the funnel. Once it was caught, he could then rush in and kill it. I sat on the floor dutifully holding up the cushions for the funnel. I also made sure that I was armed with a sandal just in case the rat tried to break the rules by jumping over the barrier. Knowing how these situations can sometimes go, I was not going to be caught unprepared.

Csaba started the operation by flushing the rat out from under the sofa. Everything went as planned when the rat took off along the wall and toward the funnel. Then it happened: the old rat broke the rules and jumped the barrier, and in doing so, he ran straight at me and onto my lap. I screeched and started furiously hitting my lap and the floor with my sandal. With my nerves being as they were, my aim was poor and I missed all my shots. The rat got away.

"Oh! He got away," commented the Conductor of Affairs, "Come on, let's put up the funnel and try again." His technician had other ideas. Since the unwillingness of this technician to prop up the rattrap a second time threatened to stop all further works, we had to resort to other means, and a complicated support system was made from cushions and toys. Eventually we did get the rat, but I am not afraid to admit that rat-catching is not my cup of tea.

But it would not be the last time Csaba or I encountered furry things in odd places. Csaba's turn came next. He was sitting on the grass talking to our translator, Alexis, while my pet mongoose (appropriately named Goose), was digging for grubs at his feet. It was an idyllic day and the sun shone down softly in the late afternoon. Suddenly the reverie was shattered when our dog came bounding around the corner and saw the mongoose. These two have had a long-standing feud and when Goose saw her antagonist coming, she wasn't going to hang around for another unpleasant encounter, so she shot into the nearest available dark hole— up the leg of Csaba's pants. The dog lunged after her but stopped short in confusion when she disappeared into the pants. He stayed sitting there, his head stupidly cocked, tongue happily hanging, and tail eagerly wagging in anticipation of more mongoose-chasing fun.

Csaba, feeling a mongoose crawling up his leg, did a very sensible thing: he put his hands firmly around his leg to stop her from getting any higher. This stopped her but did not dislodge her. There was no way she would expose her furry self to the whining idiot whose hot breath was just outside the denim barrier. Since it became clear that she intended to stay there for the day, Csaba stood up to try to shake her down. This was enough to cause Goose, who has lightning-quick reflexes, to go higher still. When Csaba realized her intentions, he tried to block her again with his hands but he was too late. She was now lodged far up in the thigh of his pants, and evidently had plans to go higher still. Csaba tried to push her down but this only made her growl.

Since she was wedged in there pretty tightly and had no intention of coming out, Csaba had a problem on his hands. His repeated attempts to push her down only caused his jeans to growl all the more. Finally I was called onto the scene to extract my mongoose from his leg as quickly as possible. I reached up from the cuff, grabbed her tail, and pulled hard. Goose didn't like this and protested vehemently while digging in her claws. I refused to give in to her and pulled even harder until I felt her give. She has very long claws used for digging grubs and she used those claws liberally all the way down. When we finally got her out, she was thankfully no worse for the wear, though the same could not be said for Csaba's leg. He has since learned not to sit down in the grass when a mongoose is about.

We have squirmed in the past, and will do so again in the future, because Africa is just "that type of place." Since we work in "that type of place," we will always be meeting with unpleasant, jumpy situations. They are just some of the occupational hazards in the life of an African missionary. In our work we are called by many names: translator, pastor and missionary; but for now just call us "Squirming in Africa."

8

The Pig Dig

Andreas and Jeremiah, our younger sons, work on their archeological digs back at the far end of the property under a thick clump of bamboo. It is a wild-looking place on the edge of nowhere, surrounded by the thick tangled bush that extends indefinitely beyond. In the middle of it there is a clearing where Noai has a small carrot garden she is always fussing over in attempts to coax her undersized carrots on to greater vigor. She never realized that nearby those innocent carrots was once, long ago, a fully-functioning civilization. Just off the east corner of the carrot bed, in the soil under the weeds and tangle of bamboo roots, was a treasure of the most precious kind. This was the location of the archeological dig directed by Dr. Andreas and his willing assistant, Jeremiah.

Dr. Andreas knew that there was an old pig farm of sorts there about five years ago, so he decided to uncover what artifacts he could by digging down in the soft dirt and into the realm of the ancient pigs. On one corner of the dig he unearthed a few cement troughs that were still in fairly good condition. Dr. Andreas surmised that this must have been how those in the ancient world ate their meals. With more effort, the doctor and his assistant dug down to the side of the troughs and found crumbled earthen walls—the ancient living quarters where the inhabitants must have slept. Across from these rooms the archeologist discovered an old cement walkway, its foundation cracked but still intact, which could only have been some type of courtyard. At the other side of the clearing was an old earthen well filled with bamboo leaves. Its mud bricks circled down a few feet until the leaves covered over all remaining traces of its depths. Dr. Andreas concluded that at some time in the past this civilization had truly flourished.

The most exciting find was yet to come. The team discovered, under the debris and leaves, the bones of some past inhabitant—yes, real bones! Think of it! The ancient pig bones, consisting of a few shankpieces and some other oddments, were painstakingly brushed off with one of Daddy's paintbrushes and collected in an ancient metal bowl (another relic of the dig). These rare bones were then proudly brought up to the house and displayed to me, the curator.

As the team examined all this evidence they wondered what life was like when pigs had roamed our corner of the earth. They noted some of the leg bones had been hacked in two (a common butchering practice here). What grim melee could have occurred to destroy these inhabitants, that their bones would be so hacked? A battle, perhaps? One could only surmise. When the analysis was over, Dr. Andreas classified his precious stash and stored it in the courtyard, as is the usual practice for archeological finds. But a week later the plot thickened when a disappointed Andreas found that all his bones were gone. Could they have been stolen? (Actually, a worker had probably thrown them out when he was sweeping the yard of trash.) Nothing could be done but to schedule another dig to unearth more bones.

When the dig is finished, Dr. Andreas and his assistant will make a report of their findings and try to reconstruct what a pig might have looked like five years ago when the civilization was at its height. I wish them luck in their future research. There is treasure everywhere.

9

The Eclipse

We were listening to a sermon tape from our home church one Sunday evening when we heard yelling coming from the village. We stopped to listen. The noise seemed to escalate in intensity and travel around to every corner of the village like a distant waterfall that was slowly beginning to flow and gather force during a heavy rain. Listening carefully, I began to recognize other sounds in the background as well: sounds of clanging and beating, and the loud thundering boom of the Bakwé drums, which are played with such intensity that they seem to take the breath away from anyone close to them.

Then, listening more intently, I picked up the soft, beautiful, almost surreal tinkling of the *balafones* (marimbas) coming from across the road on the Burkinabé side of the village. These instruments have always intrigued me with their deep rich tone that somehow seems to sing several different rhythms all at once. When you are listening to a *balafone*, the melody comes to life like some mischievous elf, taking on form and body to dance and twirl you across the night air; it brings you down again slowly and stops, only to lift you up in its arms once more in a night-long rhythm of rest and motion.

Hearing all this, Csaba told Hans to go outside and take a look at the moon. He yelled back, "Hey, the moon looks strange. Come out and see it!" Csaba told the kids to go out for a look. Eclipses of the moon do not happen often here. Csaba got out the telescope and came outside to join us. Heavily doused with insect repellent, we all sat on the soft grass and gazed up at the hazy, reddish body of the moon hanging in the night sky. Csaba fussed with the telescope and finally had it set up. All the children looked at the moon and were awed at one the marvels of this universe that God has fashioned. The villagers were looking too, but they attributed the eclipse to other reasons (the spirits covering the moon), and custom dictated that they make noise—any kind of noise—until the moon showed its full color again. Silently we watched the brightness come back to a thin crescent of the moon until slowly it was completely bathed in light once more.

At this point the clanging began to stop just in the same way it had started, a little at first and then slowly, person by person and drum by drum, dropping out until all was silent again except for the *balafones*, which kept playing and dancing into the night.

10
Hunting

Hunting is a tricky sport when you are a boy and cannot have a real gun. Repeated attempts to shoot things in the bush with homemade bows and padded arrows have proven fruitless, and when a hunter is frustrated, he will want to shoot anything—just to do it. Our dog and chickens provided ample prey for a time, but there were certain drawbacks, the main one being the dog. Our old dog took a particular liking to the padded arrows and made off with most of them. On top of that, he would not give them back when asked but insisted on a rip-roaring game of chase. This was quite annoying to Andreas and Jeremiah, who were only in the mood for hunting big game and not chasing slobbering fools. The other drawback was that the chickens became a bit more hysterical than usual and harder to catch, but it's the price one must pay for a good hunt.

Then came the wonderful day when our African worker showed Andreas how to make a spring trap out of a green branch. The two went back into the bush and found a perfect branch, bent it over, and attached a string with a noose on it. The noose was then attached to a trigger that the unsuspecting animal would step on to get at the food, which would set off the trap. The idea was sensational but reality proved to be less so: days and days of looking at the series of scattered traps provided no bush meat.

Disappointed hunters were again thinking about shooting the fool dog and our flock of now-calm chickens. Since I was curious about the traps, I went over to one and tried to spring it. It didn't spring. I tapped it. It still didn't respond. I was beginning to understand the problem of the empty game traps. Finally I whacked the trigger with some force, and it flew up in grand style to catch the empty air. So that was it—only a rather large, heavy animal could spring that trap—a trap meant for ground hogs. The very large animal would have to have a brain the size of a pea to be stupid enough to enter the trap under those conditions. Repeated attempts to fine-tune the traps only caught one animal, our little red hen that happened to have the misfortune of trying to find breakfast in the bush that day. She was not known for her intelligence or (being of the short, heavy, dumpy type) for her lightness of foot.

The boys went back to their homemade bamboo bows and arrows and finally found success. After repeated attempts to hunt for wild animals, dogs, and chickens, they shot, killed, skinned, and ate a wild grapefruit. Stationary prey is always so much easier to shoot than a moving one, and though I don't mind them killing an occasional grapefruit or two, all their shots left holes in the few remaining good ones on the tree.

In addition to the new sport of fruit-shooting, they found another quarry which is a bit out of the ordinary and quite elusive. With this new quarry they used more sophisticated means—bows and arrows and spring traps were of no use here. They now hunted with a hound (my mongoose), and their prey were giant crickets. African giant crickets are about two inches in length and have legs as long as my little finger. They dig deep tunnels and make a deafening noise at night which I would rather do without. When you get near them they will escape deep down their holes so they are difficult to catch. To catch them the hunters go out at night with a flashlight in one hand and my fat hound, Goose, tucked away carelessly in the other.

Tramping in the dark with their flashlights, the kids will follow the loud sounds of a cricket until they come to the general vicinity of the noise. Then they turn their heads back and forth to locate exactly where the sound is coming from. Once they have found the hole, they will release my mongoose. She will dig at a determined and frantic pace, grunting and whistling with excitement. After she has almost disappeared down the hole she will triumphantly bring up a mouthful of cricket, with the "drumsticks" dangling out of the sides of her mouth. We then get to watch her thoroughly enjoy her meal, complete with warning growls to ward us off, just in case we had any thought of sharing this delicacy with her. When that's done, the hound, still smacking her lips, is collected back up in the arms of the hunters and they all go off to find another hole.

I have no idea what sort of animal they will pursue next. I have no idea whether one day I will walk back on our property and find myself dangling by one foot in a tree, or looking up out of a ten-foot panther pit. When a hunter is determined enough, anything can happen, and I have to keep a vigilant watch. I only wish they would use their hunting skills in the house to catch the mice. Now *there's* a worthwhile quarry.

11
Mice

We indeed have a multitude of creatures here, most of them unwanted—at least inside the house. Sometimes we have bouts with particularly troublesome resident mice. These mice are smart and difficult to catch; compared to their stateside cousins, African mice are real professionals. Traps do not often work on them. If Csaba baits a trap with banana, the banana will be gone the next morning and the trap left unsprung. Csaba thought at first that the problem lay with the traps themselves, but he found out differently when he touched one lightly and it immediately snapped shut on his finger. I often wonder how the mice evade them. We even put a piece of banana in a plastic bag and then *tied* it onto the trap, but believe it or not, some little Houdini chewed through the bag and ate the banana, leaving the trap still unsprung. Finally we just had to give up and cope as best we could.

Csaba has a lot of tolerance (which I do not share) for mice running around the kitchen or in the living room, but when it comes to his books—it's another story. One mouse had the audacity to chew on one of the precious books that Csaba kept over his desk. That was the last straw. Out came the trap again; maybe, just maybe, it would work this time. He located the place where he thought the mouse was scaling the heights, under the desk by a board that was attached to the bookcase. As we should have anticipated, the mouse was suspicious of the trap and bypassed it for another route up the shelves. The loaded mousetrap was soon forgotten until, of course, Csaba inadvertently put his toe on it while he was working on his computer and nearly went through the ceiling. I am certain a mouse was laughing from behind an analytical Greek New Testament at the misfortune of his would-be pursuer.

Csaba was not the only one inconvenienced by the mouse. The children and I were having a peaceful school session one morning about to do our science project on human anatomy when Hans suddenly called out, "Mom, there's a mouse in the Invisible Man box!" I jumped up and ran to the box, but it was too late and the little villain got away. I looked inside the box and saw the instructions to my Invisible Man made into a nice nest. In the nest were shredded diagrams of kidneys and lungs and the names of the bones. I was mortified. What use is an Invisible Man if I didn't know the names of all his parts? Why couldn't the mouse have made his nest in the scrap bin? I set down the box with new determination. We were going to get that mouse.

I gave out orders to block all exits and stationed the kids around the room to flush the little beast out. I had to take half of my books and school supplies from the shelves to get him to show himself, but he did. He flew out in a panic, made a loop around the school table, and darted back onto the bookshelves and hid there again. This time I removed all the puzzles, crafts and games and put them on the floor. Only a few books remained.

Now exposed, the mouse shot out again and dashed to the other side of the room like a ricocheting bullet. The kids started yelling directions to each other, and whoever wasn't yelling was stomping wildly. It didn't work. The mouse shot back into the almost bare shelves. This time I removed the last of the books—my precious science books. I now had piles of stuff all over the floor: books, games, puzzles and odd bits of my Invisible Man's parts scattered here and there. I also had the kids stationed on chairs and various other spots of the room with shoes in their hands when Csaba entered and gave me a quizzical look. He never knows quite what to expect from his sedate wife and today was no exception. I responded casually that we were out to avenge my invisible man for his shredded instructions. Csaba just smiled and walked on.

Finally we were able to scare the mouse out to the living room and behind a box. All the kids were yelling and swinging their shoes. Now that we had him terrified and cornered, I called in our outdoor worker to catch him, which he did, and then took him outside to feed his pet crocodile. Another of my arch-nemeses had finally met its demise.

12

The Secret Garden

Though the fig trees do not blossom, nor fruit be on the vines, the produce of the olive fail and the fields yield no food, the flock be cut off from the fold and there be no herd in the stalls, yet I will rejoice in the Lord, I will joy in the God of my salvation. (Hab. 3:17–18)

Noai likes to garden. So do I, but it can be discouraging if one actually wants to eat fresh produce. My efforts receive, on the average, about a twenty percent yield on all crops not native to this soil. When I put in a vegetable garden in the rainy season, the snails eat the young shoots until not a single one is left. I tried the old beer-in-a-dish trick but found out African snails are veritable teetotalers refusing to oblige and drown themselves in the beer as they are supposed to do. What does not meet its demise by snails, by some miracle, will get the rot. What doesn't get the rot will be damaged by nematodes. Nematodes are remedied by companion planting with marigolds, but the snails love marigolds like candy, and when the marigolds are eaten to the ground by the snails, the beans die of nematode invasions and I am back to square one. So much for the wet season. If I wait until dry season, the locusts come out and chew artistic patterns in the leaves until the plants are virtually leafless.

Once I had the ingenious idea of starting my garden mid-season. It was doing well until the chickens found it and uprooted the whole thing looking for grubs. I tried shutting up the chickens but they were adamant against this limitation on their freedom. When there is a will to escape, there is always a way. Determined to actually have a workable garden and foil the chickens, I transferred the whole operation to the little islands in the swamp behind our ponds. Here the snails couldn't get to it and the chickens couldn't find it, but the pigs did when they escaped from their pen and chose my beds to wallow in, and that was the end of it. All in all, I keep thinking that I should give up on serious gardening except for the standard African fare of rice, fruit trees, corn, manioc, yams, okra and sweet potatoes. Maybe next year I'll have another go.

Even if I have nearly given up on gardening, Noai has not. Hers is no ordinary garden. She decided to take a different approach than my ill-fared attempts at vegetables: she made herself a hidden tropical garden. She first enlisted her big brother to do the machete work in the back passages of the bush. Hans chopped out a tunnel into the wall of solid green that borders our paths, making the passageway wind around a few turns before opening up into a dome-like interior deep in the thick jungle. There he cleared the earth of debris, leaving a round, tent-sized space canopied by a vaulted ceiling of living green, several feet of tangled leaves that touched the open sky above. It was beautiful and almost like another secret world where little flecks of light fell down onto the dark, damp surface of the jungle floor.

When the clearing work was finished, she dug up from our yard various shade-loving plants that one might see in a flower shop in the tropical section back in the States. In her secret garden there is a forest lily that blooms large, white Easter lilies twice a year. There are several caladiums, their elephant ears dotted with their own red and white paint in intricate patterns. She planted a spider orchid against one of the small trees on the wall of her dome. There is a shade-loving philodendron with such delicate stripes of white and pink it's as if some fairy painted them on. To one side is a thin-leafed plant, dark purple like a plum. Ferns and ornamental vines are planted all around on the edges of her space where the dome of green meets the damp earth. Noai has the ability to see beauty where others see only tangled bush, and to create beauty where before it didn't exist. Every flower in the garden seems to be hers by right, every soft delicate plant rendered for her sensitive touch to do as she pleases. Noai is responsible for gardens suddenly popping up on our property in the most unexpected places.

For a finishing touch she made a stool of concrete bricks and wooden boards and put it in the middle of the dome, where she can steal away, sit

46

still, and silently watch the forest life from a hidden vantage point. I can walk right by this section of the bush and not know she is there.

When I finally saw the secret garden I was enchanted, but the only thing I could say to her was, "This is wonderful. But watch out for snakes. A large cobra was spotted here the other day." (That is all I ever seem to say to my kids. "Have fun. Watch out for snakes," or "Don't climb too high this time, and watch out for snakes." They put up with me anyhow.)

It is beautiful and peaceful in the secret garden. The leaves drip with the light rains and the earth smells of living things. There the busy world is shut out by a mystical realm that is all its own. She's learned one doesn't have to be a vegetable gardener to attain some success. One just has to pick the right type of garden for the right type of climate—the right type of garden, that is, for a rain forest.

But then again I mustn't give up on my vegetables. I am determined I shall get a crop somehow. I am already on my third attempt at lettuce. If I can only get some nets to stop the locusts, or maybe dig a moat around my raised beds to stop the snails, or plant more marigolds next to the beans, or light a fire to keep away the rot and the chickens, or enlist Hans to wield his catapult against the pigs, just maybe this time it will at last grow and flourish.

As you work on your garden this year, take some time to thank God for it, but do not feel sorry for me. If I get discouraged when I want to eat from my garden (I now buy vegetables in the city and freeze them), I can always concentrate on the fruit. We have no problem with fruit. In my garden I have mango, guava, grapefruit, orange, lime, mandarin, papaya, false almond and other nuts, banana, plantain banana, cape cherry, passion fruit, tropical mulberry, bread fruit, custard apple, sour sop, water apple, coconut, sugar cane, cocoa, palm nut, and tons and tons of juicy, sweet pineapple. We too have a lot to be thankful for.

13
Noai

There are certain fleeting moments in time that, if stopped and held, say so much about a person—actions that bring a personality to life and render it special. I love to capture such moments, no matter how small or mundane, like a camera imprinting a scene and immortalizing it forever in my mind.

She came into my room with a handful of newly-hatched chicks she was now "mom" to. Her hands had dirt on them and under the fingernails from digging in the soft earth of her garden. Her skirt was stained and her hair had a wild look, wild with the wind and the sun and much free time out in the open tropical air. She came to tell me something important, so she plopped down on our waterbed to say what was on her mind. Her plop started a wave underneath the sheets which rolled away from her, hit the headboard, then made its way back. As she was collecting her thoughts, her head rose and fell with the waves, but she seemed not to notice. In the meantime two chicks had stolen their way out of her hands and onto the bed. The chicks had trouble keeping their balance on the waterbed, so she scooped them back up and clutched them more tightly in her skirt.

She began to tell me of the discovery she had made. "Mom, do you know those curly snails that look like a roasted bun all twirled up? Well, if you look at one real carefully, you'll see veins running all along on the shell and you can actually see the heart pumping!"

Then she bounded out of my sphere and into hers again; her chicks were complaining and she had to put them to bed. As she left, another wave swept over the bed, only to rebound again into nothingness.

14

"Civilizations"

It was a new morning and I was out in it, enjoying its beauty and walking in the mist. There is always a mist as the sun is coming up over the horizon. It gives the trees a ghostly look and the ground a haziness that washes all colors into one. I walked down to the pond and saw little streams of vapor floating up like steam from a simmering caldron. The trees above were dripping back their dew, breaking the pond's placid surface with ringlets forming a hundred little circles that spread and faded out into calm water. As I was admiring all of this beauty, I stumbled upon, to my surprise, a miniature town nestled down in the old garden plot between the roses and my raised flowerbeds, looking alone and abandoned like an ancient relic of ages past.

What was this place and who were its people? I stood like Gulliver among the Lilliputians. This town was made of hard clay dried in the sun, causing little cracks to form and spread all across the walls and roofs of the tiny buildings. As I looked along the rustic streets and clay buildings, I noticed the town was not only built practically, but architecturally beautiful too. The buildings were designed in a Greek style, and great care had been taken to add porcelain facades and alabaster roofs by using clays of different colors.

The builder of this city wanted to have a full array of protection for its people. It had advanced barracks for its soldiers and an armory filled with clay catapults. There was even a trireme ship built out of palm ribs overlaid with paper. Its exactness to the original was amazing for something so small.

Of course the town had a treasury—a very fascinating building indeed. Its outside steps led into an open-faced structure with treasures stacked safely inside. I peeked in to see what type of treasures could be there and found bits of gold and silver paper crumpled up into ingots.

My eye wandered past the treasury to the other structures of the city. The general store was a simple building filled with clay vats carefully carved and filled with a reddish substance, a kind of wine made from crushed rose petals. More petals were neatly stacked off to the side, ready to be pressed.

On glancing around, I noticed there was no proper palace for the king. I found out later the king had to be content with sleeping in the temple, which wasn't so bad. The great temple had pillars adorning its entrance and broad steps leading up to the door. Inside was a beautiful clay altar made of a rare, white clay. Stored in the same room were rolled up scrolls of dried banana leaves with the history of the civilization written upon them.

I left the city and wandered across the countryside of this miniature world. On the outskirts were farms dotted here and there with rows of scattered crops. Beyond the farms, in the 'wild bush,' was an ancient ziggurat that stood ominously clothed in deteriorating grandeur. Inside its clay depths, sealed for all eternity, lay a small tomb. In it was a buried scroll made of banana leaf with the history of the deceased king written on it. That was not all—on a parchment were the directions for finding the treasure buried deep within the clay tunnels.

I decided to leave the "Hanzite" civilization and the ghosts of its past, and followed a little sandy road that wound away from the ziggurat, in and out of a tangle of weeds. Along its border was a watchtower that told me I was leaving one kingdom and entering another. I followed the road for a long time until I again came upon some small farms. These farms were different from the Hanzite farms, in that they had been fashioned in an incredible amount of detail. One farm was situated by a small "lake." On the lake were a couple of boats made of old cocoa pods cut in half, attached to a dock among the reeds. The farm had a little thatched cottage with a picturesque fence surrounding it and inside the fence were pens for animals and a garden. In the garden flowers were growing next to rows of brightly colored green crops. It was such a peaceful, domestic scene I knew for certain its inhabitants were very happy.

The civilization apparently did not fear invasion because barracks and war machines were almost nonexistent. Instead it had a wonderful palace of exquisite beauty where the royal couple lived in style. (*They* would not be banished to the temple.) The town had a bountiful market, filled with heaps of baby avocadoes, limes, coffee beans, and grains of various types. There were small seeds that looked like pumpkins. A stack of deep purple cloth made from flower petals lay under a shelter, ready to be exported. Bell flowers were used as water basins. I could see this town specialized in food, while the Hanzite capital which I had so recently left had only wine for its people to survive on.

With some effort I left the civilization, which called itself "Minoan," and headed for a third and smaller civilization by a stand of bamboo overshadowing the pond. This civilization specialized in the fishing trade. The whole appearance of the town was one of neatness and orderliness, expressed in its two barracks, temple, and single house. The rest of the people, I understood, were confined in one large apartment building just outside of town. The house must have been for the king, for I saw no palace—obviously an unnecessary luxury. The armory had cut up snail parts drying on the roof. What benefit could snail parts be to the army? I could not guess, and I doubted the army would use them— instead they would be used for fishing bait by the town's maker later in the afternoon. The other notable feature was a central square graced with two clay statues of lions that could be mistaken for dogs. There was also the bountiful supply of ice cream cones, the town's major source of food and export.

The last civilization I came across was situated by the overflow section of the main pond. Next to the cascading waterfall that came off the pipe was a sort of outpost or robber's den resting on a mud hill in the middle of several pools of water of varying heights. It was not an elaborate operation at all. The pools were hand dug and contained a few tadpoles and some frogs, which seemed to be the only occupants of the place. Off to the side, a miniature stone's throw away, a fishing pole was lying in the grass.

Since it now started to rain, I moved on past the "Jeremiad" outpost, and as I walked in the grass toward the second pond, I saw Hans bent over a little fishing village he was in the process of creating. His long arms and legs were stuffed in a raincoat that had in years past engulfed him, but was now much too small. He was bent over his town, intent on the last finishing touches.

"What are you writing down?" he said.

I told him I was recording all that he and the others had created in their civilizations, and how he had masterminded the whole operation. I told him one day he would forget about all of this, and my notes would be a good record for future generations.

He stood there and said reflectively, "I guess some day I'll be too old to be doing this sort of thing."

"I don't think you'll ever be too old to create," I responded. "Somehow, in some way, you'll always be creating things." He nodded his assent and turned back to his miniature world now being soaked with the rain. I looked to the swampy area behind the pond at the Minoan civilization with its beautiful farms and cottages and saw its creator, Noai, busy covering her world with a bit of plastic. Andreas was covering the Andreasite civilization with a mat; fishing would have to wait. The Jeremiad outpost was left standing unprotected since its maker was poking about the pond for tadpoles and couldn't be bothered by the rain. When the rain started coming down harder, I turned to go back up to the house.

Hans had not only masterminded the whole operation, but made up rules to govern the cities as well. He set up rules for trade and for what must go into the building of a new city. There were rules for conquering other civilizations and rules for getting tribute. Each civilization had a recorded history written by its creator. I only had to come in and settle an argument once, when Hans wanted to lay siege to Noai's settlement since it was so lightly defended. Noai came to me in tears and I suggested that Hans sign a treaty with her peaceable folk and concentrate on attacking his brothers.

The civilizations lasted for a long time until the heavy rains came and washed them into ruins and relics of the past. One day some budding archeologist may uncover the ruins and the treasure, read the histories on the scrolls, and write again what happened in days gone by, at our pond.

15

A Typical Day

Many of our friends back home wonder what happens in a "typical day" in the life of the Leidenfrosts. This is a difficult subject to write about since our life changes so much, but what follows is my attempt to sketch the outlines of a semi-typical day in our village. (Our family timeframe: Hans age ten, Noai eight, Andreas six, Jeremiah three.)

I wake up with the crowing of a cock. I look out the window; it is pitch black outside, and for all practical purposes it is still the middle of the night. After I verify the hour on my bedside clock, I find that it still *is* the middle of the night, and why is that stupid cock crowing again at such an unearthly hour? I fall back to sleep with some difficulty, only to be awakened later by the same cock. This time he is a little more accurate. The clock now reads 5:45 a.m. but it is still completely dark. When I look out the window fifteen minutes later, it is a bright sunny morning and the birds are all up and singing; being on the equator, we have no real dawn or dusk. The rooster has not ceased to tell the world how wonderful he is for the last half hour, and all his hens are clucking their agreement. Our day has begun.

When I get up, I can hear the happy chatter of the children as they do their chores. The parrot is also wide awake and talking up a storm in a language only he can decipher. Noai goes to feed her flock of chickens. Hans grabs the African broom (sticks tied together) and sweeps the living room while Andreas is busy in the bedrooms. I oversee the work of the morning and get ready for the day by writing out the various jobs for the employees. Then it is breakfast. Our choices for breakfast are usually oatmeal, granola, muffins, or biscuits. I call the kids in and we sit down to eat, but Noai is missing. I yell her name out the window. She appears from the chicken pen with a chicken in her arms and calls out, "This one is giving me trouble again. I'll be up in a minute."

We sit down to breakfast and Csaba reads a passage out of the Bible. He then dashes off to start his morning Bible study with his team back in the old office behind our house. Ten minutes later one of Csaba's guys comes in panting (he overslept again) and shoots us a quick greeting as he dashes down to the office. Five minutes later the last worker comes flying in and grins a "hello" with a guilty look as he too rushes toward the office. It is difficult to get all the guys together at once since they are on "African time," but they do enjoy Csaba's study when and if they get there, and they always say afterward how much it has helped them.

With breakfast done, the children leave to start their lessons and I talk with Javier after he comes up from the study. Javier is simply beaming as usual and gives me a hearty greeting. I tell him the work of the day and let him go. Then I try to find Bibionay, my outdoor worker, who can chop down a swath of bush with his machete faster than anyone I know (except Javier). He also washes our mud-stained clothes by hand until they are spotless. The advantage of having Bibionay rather than a machine is that he doesn't break down, doesn't require electricity, and he redoes things that are not quite clean. He also laughs and smiles and generally has a cheerful attitude toward life, unlike our current washing machine (we finally got one later when electricity came to the village), which breaks down constantly and seems to have a chronic bad attitude.

After pulling away from the circle of men in the Bible study, Csaba goes up to eat breakfast with his Bakwé team to talk over the work of the day. This also turns into counseling time if one of the guys is having a problem that needs to be addressed. Javier and Bibionay don't sit down for coffee and prefer to have theirs on the run. We let all our workers have free access to the coffee and sugar, though they will incredibly finish off a whole bowl of sugar in a day. They put an average of seven spoons of sugar into their coffee—that is the African way. When breakfast is over, Csaba and Alexis go down to the office to start work on the computer.

When I finish speaking with Javier and Bibionay, I come back to check the children's work and then start teaching one child at a time while the others are set up to do their work alone. At this point I could be called to greet someone outside or pulled over to be asked more questions by our workers, or we might all stop to watch a snake-kill. No day is quite like the others. At mid-morning I do a short devotional with the kids and then we take a break. We love to walk out in our five acres and enjoy its beauty. We first check the chickens to see if there are any new eggs laid or chicks hatched. Then we go to the back to check the orchard for any ripe fruit. There is usually some type of fruit ripe all year round that we can enjoy for a snack.

Frogs are Andreas's specialty. When we reach the frog pond Andreas yells, "There's a big one, mama! Let's get the butterfly net and catch him!" As I gingerly make my way along the pond's muddy banks in search of the elusive bullfrog, our large and rather clumsy dog comes bounding out of the brush and splashes into the water. This makes catching frogs rather difficult since "Ol' Fuzz-Face" insists on engaging me in a game of throw-the-stick-in-the-pond. I appease the dog while Noai is at the other end looking for tadpoles.

Hans goes to check on his mud bricks drying in the sun. He now has more than a hundred handmade bricks, with which he hopes to raise the walls of his mud house a little bit higher. I call the kids over and we start our school time again under the mango tree, swinging in the hammocks. This is my favorite place to read to them.

When we finish a chapter, we head back to the house, where the kids assemble around me for a history lesson. This proves difficult when the parrot starts talking as soon as I do. I will often put a cloth over his cage and tell him he is a noisy bird and ought to be quiet. Sometimes I'll hear a little voice coming from under the cloth saying, 'Noisy bird, noisy bird." If the parrot is extra sassy and starts shrieking, I remove his cage to the bathroom and close the door. Once I forgot him in there and when I walked by much later I heard a muffled voice say, "Good morning, bird!"

Meanwhile Csaba is finishing a cultural write-up on Bakwé funerals, helping Alexis with problems on the computer, and checking the texts Alexis is working on for the grammar paper. He is in the middle of it all when he is interrupted by a call from Javier to come and greet some visitors who wish to see him. Csaba goes to the porch to talk to them until he is interrupted by Alexis. Evidently another computer problem has suddenly cropped up; these seem to be a rather frequent occurrence with our team. Csaba and Alexis say goodbye to the visitors and go to see what horrors the computer has produced to torment them this time.

It is time for lunch and we go up to the dining area in our kitchen house. If someone is visiting with Csaba at the moment, we will invite him in to eat. Our lunch consists of rice with some type of sauce; usually there is smoked fish with it and occasionally we eat one of the young cocks—with the kids' permission. Before I began to raise fryers as a special breed, we would eat the excess off our village flock, but this proved a bit difficult at times since the chickens had all become our kids' friends. Inevitably, as I would hold out a young rooster for eating approval, Noai would quietly say, "But mama, *that* is Louis." How can one eat a rooster named Louis? I wish she would be content to name the hens and leave the eatables comfortably anonymous.

Speaking of roosters, our red rooster Henry usually shows up at noon for a snack. I am in the kitchen getting things ready when I hear some scratching at the kitchen door, and sure enough it is Henry, bobbing his head and looking up at me with his hungry chicken eyes, waiting for some rice. We like to indulge him, which is why he keeps coming around at noon and blocking the screen door.

After lunch, Hans studies Latin with Csaba and I help Noai get started on her piano lessons. I put Jeremiah down for his nap and take my own "nap" too, which consists of reading a book alone. When the kids have finished their homework, they run out into the yard—Hans to raise his house a few more layers with Anay, one of his Bakwé friends; Noai to check on the chicken pen; Andreas to build with his Legos. Bibionay comes back from his lunch break and I take him out to the garden to give him his instructions for the remainder of the afternoon. Depending upon the day, I will either do garden work with the kids or go visiting in the village with Noai. Csaba is still working in the office with Alexis, poring over some linguistic data.

One part of our routine that rarely changes comes at about four o'clock when the village children come. I know that they have arrived when I hear their soft little voices and giggles, and when I look out the window I see a whole row of smiling faces. I greet them and they greet me back.

They ask for the kids and I call them up to play. Hans runs toward the flame tree with the boys to play soccer. Andreas brings out our dilapidated toy trucks, relics of Csaba's childhood, and the younger kids will roll them recklessly around the yard. A very old tricycle with one wheel missing is brought out to be rolled around or dragged down our sandy driveway. Noai will sometimes play by herself or will skip rope with the girls from the village if they come. They make a rather noisy, rowdy lot, but they do have fun together.

In the meantime, more visitors come to see Csaba and this time he is called into the village to visit a sick person. He may be asked later to drive them to the clinic or to get medicine in town. At five o'clock, Csaba returns but he is called off once again into the village to see to another problem. I start dinner and give out bandages to any village kids that need them, along with many drinks of water and occasionally some fruit. I send them all home with happy hearts, and my kids go in and take their bucket baths, which they do by dipping hot water out of our huge kettles on the mud stove, then adding well water from the barrel in the kitchen. At about this time the sky darkens and a late afternoon storm begins to brew. As night falls and the storm is coming on, Javier slips out the door and into the churning night to return home with his brother.

We eat dinner with the rain beating down hard on the tin roof. It is difficult to talk during this time unless you prefer to shout. When dinner is over and the storm has abated, we sit down to our family worship time. The hymnals come out and everyone joins in singing with a joyful heart—even the parrot perched rather smugly on Csaba's shoulders. All together we can make quite a din. Afterwards we read the Bible and pray, and then comes bedtime with all the cuddles and singing that go with it.

After the kids are in bed, Csaba and I will finally have a chance to talk about the day's happenings. We light the kerosene lanterns for a night-light, let down the mosquito nets over the beds, and settle down for the night. Another day has just gone by.

16

A Tropical Storm

In the cycle of our year we have only dry seasons and wet seasons. The most intense sun comes in the spring and fall, triggering powerful storms as the season changes. The spring storms settle into a rainy summer season, followed by a dry August and September. October brings the fall storms which then fade into another dry season. I love the storms that come in these changing times of the year, but especially at the end of February when the winter dry season breaks and the desert winds are swept back again over the Sahara. There are many fierce storms, setting our world in violent motion, seemingly shaking it from top to bottom. One feels so small when the power of God is unleashed on the earth.

The day starts out like any other, bright and sunny. The sun glances over the horizon and bathes the countryside in light. Small wisps of clouds hang overhead and far away on the placid horizon. The giant cottonwood trees stand calmly at the field's end like lazy giants just waking up from their slumber, rising and stretching to tower high over the other trees in the scattered forest. The jungle comes to life as birds twitter through the trees and chickens waddle around the yard to scratch for food. The village is already awake at the first cock's crow and work is in full swing. Csaba and his translators have just started their work too.

As the day moves on and the sun shines high overhead, the heat bakes the earth. All life slows down, avoiding any unnecessary movement. The world seems to go back to sleep under the blankets of a heavy, humid atmosphere. The chickens pant under the cover of the bushes, waiting for the sun to pass its zenith. Our dog digs a hole in the soft dirt and lies down in the shade. In the village there is little life; the people sit in their reclining chairs or lie on mats for a siesta, seemingly dead to the world. All is still and resting except for Csaba and his translators, who take only a short break and then are back to work, dripping with sweat, bent over their computers.

As the sun passes its zenith the sky slowly changes. The gentle clouds start to build up in layers, stacking one on top of another like frosted billowy cakes until they reach a tremendous height. The tops of these newly formed towers are caught by the wind and swept out over the sky like spilled milk. The direction of the spill tells which way the upper winds are blowing and what direction the storm is likely to take. Down below there is no wind. As the afternoon slips away towards evening, the huge towers darken.

The air in the upper atmosphere becomes confused, as if it cannot decide which direction to go. It is no longer blowing in one direction but seems to move and swirl in all directions at once. The towers of cloud on the horizon, thousands of feet high, continue to build and become blacker, revealing flashes of lightning within. The air on the ground picks up and blows into a steady wind, disturbing the placid trees. We hear a distant rumble of thunder. A solid wall of black creeps up the horizon from behind the scattered forest and the giant cottonwood trees, which stand nobly against the rising wall appear to burn in the last red rays of the sun like torches against a night's sky.

The sun goes out and a shadow falls over the land. The wind stops for a moment, an eerie quiet, the ominous calm before the storm. The birds stop chirping and fly for cover. The chickens scramble for their bedtime spots in the trees. Over in the office I can still see Csaba and the men working steadily on, completely oblivious to the changes outside.

Then as if someone turns on a switch, activating a machine that comes roaring out of the horizon, everything is set in motion. A terrific wind sweeps over the trees and flings their captive leaves into instant freedom. I can hear the village coming to life as everyone scrambles to gather laundry left on bushes and pick up piles of cocoa beans spread out to dry. I join them, madly trying to grab my laundry off the line before the rain hits. The kids and Javier rush out to help me.

I now hear in the distance a loud roar like a tidal wave rushing up from the sea and over the earth. It gets louder and louder as it crashes over the canopy of the scattered forest. The wind and rain come hurrying to ravage the land and we find ourselves caught between them; then, with incredible force, the wind and rain collide into us and the world is in instant, violent motion as winds in a howling fury toss the massive trees back and forth like rag dolls. The small black silhouettes of the chickens hang on to their pitching perches as if on a bucking horse. The dog howls pitifully under the carport, wanting in vain to be taken into the house. Rain comes in sheets that beat against the cement walls.

I rush into the house and run around the rooms trying to close the shutters against the onslaught. It has already wet the floors and cushions. The rain whips in sideways and reaches long fingers of mist across the room. The thunderous drumming on the zinc roof makes talking impossible; we shout to be heard. We start to get buckets out to collect the drips from the roof. I notice that the translators down in the office are finally aroused from their work and are shutting the doors and windows of their little world as well.

The kids and I love a good storm, and we steal out to places where we can watch the action. Hans joins me out on the front porch, which is on the lee side of the house. There we feel like we are on a boat tossed in a swirling sea with waves of rain, spitting and churning, washing in around us. Pitching trees are whipped with such violence that the whole world seems broken by their beating. I feel as if we too could be swept up in the fray and lost in the commotion.

Then there comes a time when the wind slowly starts to abate, and the violent sheets of rain lessen to a steady downpour. The lightning is still flashing dully in the distance while the thunder grumbles its parting words. The air becomes calmer as the trees settle down to receive the steady rain watering the ground. Ever so slowly, the rain lessens and then stops. The sun breaks out from behind the passing clouds. The drenched and pathetically bedraggled chickens get down from their trees to look for a few last grubs before the evening steals in. The storm has lasted less than an hour.

I open the shutters and notice the men in the office opening their shutters too. They have probably worked right through the storm. I hear stirrings in the village again where the women begin steadily pounding yams for the evening meal. The earth is calm once more.

Part III
Village Life

We like our work. I know many people who feel a calling to ministry are always praying to God, "Please don't send me to Africa," as if that were the ultimate punishment or purification one could endure. We on the other hand are very thankful for our opportunity to live here; we feel we are the privileged ones, some of the few who are allowed to partake in such an exciting life with such an important task. In this life there is always something going on, something new we are learning, something interesting to be discovered and recorded. Life is never boring—in fact, it can be almost too exciting.

17

Alexis' Wedding

I love weddings. Weddings are exciting enough for me in the States, but they are even more so here in Africa because I never know what to expect. Our translator Alexis' wedding was no exception, and it was even more special to us because it was the very first all-Bakwé, Christian wedding we had ever heard of. We hope there will be many more in the future, and each one will be fresh and new.

In some ways weddings in Ivory Coast, due to the French influence, are very similar to weddings I have seen in the States. The parents give the bride away, a choir sings, and a pastor preaches a message. There are the vows, the ring, the kiss, and the customary eating of the cake. But in this wedding, there were many more things that struck me as different. Since I have not attended many weddings here, I am not sure if these things were unique to this wedding or if they were typical of most weddings in Ivory Coast.

One universal constant in all cultures seems to be the elaborate preparation of the bride. Alexis' bride was no exception. Marie was already a beautiful woman. She had lustrous, wide-set eyes set off by a softly curved forehead which gave her eyes a lovely, dreamy look. For the wedding her hair was intricately sculpted by adding dark and bronze strands of false hair that coiled and swirled up high on her head. The bronze strands formed little curls on the sides of her head and were highlighted by a touch of bright glitter. Her white dress made a striking contrast to her rich, molasses-colored skin. When the light shone down on her face it gave her natural highlights on her cheeks and brows. There are few things more stunning than an African woman dressed up all in white. Where the white ends and the dark begins there are such vivid lines, one more brilliant contrast in a place that seems to be defined by brilliant contrasts.

Yet another contrast: the groom. Alexis remained his same, familiar self in a simple African print shirt and khakis. He looked much excited by it all but was trying not to show it.

Before the wedding could begin, the "sponsor" had to arrive. It is common in this region for the groom to pick a sponsor for the wedding. The person chosen is usually some kind of important social or political figure whom the couple wishes to honor at the wedding. He often backs the festivities financially if the mood is upon him. Of course everyone expects the mood will be upon him; why else would they have asked him in the first place? Csaba had hoped to dispense with the sponsor because it turns the focus of the wedding from celebrating the couple to honoring the sponsor, but the time did not yet seem right to give up this important custom.

In many cases, having a sponsor is a political move to gain favor with him. It is thus impossible for the wedding to take place without him, since he might be offended. So everyone must wait for his bidding. Once a sponsor actually called off the wedding the morning it was to take place because he had to fly to Europe on short notice. We could not avoid having this story in mind when Alexis' sponsor called up and said that he was on his way back from Abidjan and would be two hours late. In Africa, when you say two hours you could mean six, or worse yet, the next day. But nobody seemed to mind the wait except the groom, who was now looking anxious but trying not to show it.

We breathed a sigh of relief when we got news several hours later that the sponsor had finally arrived. When we arrived at the church, the building was already crowded. It was quite incredible just how many people could be stuffed into a small church which already contained a large choir, a full instrumental group, four pastors, and several photographers. We put on a brave face and entered the fray. We were escorted to the front and shown two large padded chairs to sit on—places of honor. The sponsor also had a place of honor. We were fortunate to be in the front since we would have surely suffocated in the heat among the masses of bodies packed tightly together in the back. It occurred to me that our kids were all back there; I wondered how they were doing.

The choir sang as the bride walked down the aisle. Since I could not see the bride or the aisle in the sea of people, I watched the choir, which turned out to be well worth watching. As they sang, they swayed and moved in their places with every inch of their bodies. I was fascinated. I thought of the state of atoms confined to a solid phase—they must stay in their places, yet they move. The choir did the same; their heads moved up and down, their feet moved in a two-step dance, and their hips swayed to the beat while the upswing of their elbows highlighted the offbeat. They all had to be coordinated enough to do this together, at the same time, in the same direction, or surely it would have gotten a bit ugly. It never did, and the effect was a feeling that the whole room was swaying and moving like a ship at high sea. I wanted to hold onto my chair just to remain upright.

Then, to my amazement, they all slowly disappeared as they danced, sinking behind the pews. I didn't notice it at first since they were all swaying and shaking together, but slowly, as the talking-drums thundered, the choir appeared to be getting shorter and shorter until all that I could see of them were their heads bobbing just behind the pews. Then almost imperceptibly, they reappeared again, never missing a beat. Under the combined effect of the drums, music, singing, and wild motion of bodies, I was left once again clutching my chair. I had never seen anything like it from choirs in the States (though I think they could really benefit from this maneuver). It keeps the congregation always guessing what the choir will do next.

When the bride finally emerged from the throng and found her groom, the pastor called out, "Who gives this girl away?" A deep voice from the first row said, "I do." The bride and groom sat down side by side on large, padded chairs strewn with lengths of bright African material, and the sermon began. I suppose it was a very fine sermon, though I don't remember anything of what was said. The microphone in the small room was turned up so loud it hurt my ears, and the preacher (which is typical here) was shouting into it for the entire thirty minutes. I don't know why he felt the need to shout, since we all could have heard him quite clearly if he had even just whispered into microphone. This, along with the constant talking behind me, caused all noise to become a single indistinguishable whole. My ears were throbbing. Even the bride and groom looked a bit dazed.

Suddenly I became alert. They were about to cut my cake. Yes, it was *my* cake—one of my rare attempts which somehow turned out right. They cut the cake as part of the ceremony, and the eating of it symbolized the two becoming one. In Africa, men and women do not usually eat together. To share a meal is an intimate thing and has great significance. On this solemn occasion they fed each other with a special reverence.

The vows were made with gusto. After every question asked, the respondent would belt out a strong *Oui!* Such forcefulness is customary since a half-hearted assent would be a sign of hesitation. In a culture where people can be pressured and even forced to marry, everyone wants to know that the bride feels the same way about the proceedings as the groom does.

After the vows, as in American weddings, it was time for the groom to kiss the bride. Alexis reached over and brushed his cheek against Marie's on both sides in the French fashion. That was the "acceptable" kiss. He looked at her and smiled, wanting to kiss her on the mouth, which is rather bold for Africa. She looked down shyly and he had to raise her chin to kiss her. The whole church erupted into hooting. The choir burst out of their "solid" chemical state and instantly melted into a completely liquid one, atoms running and moving, struggling to go faster but always slowed by bumping into others. The now exuberantly dancing choir had, in their excitement, spilled out of their pews and into the front, dancing circles around the star-struck couple. Others from the audience immediately rushed to join the dance, and the room became awash with enthusiastic and happy movement. The couple did not seem to notice, still dazed from the kiss. They just stood staring at each other. We in the meantime kept being jostled by the dancers as they went by.

The whole place was in joyful pandemonium. The bride and groom, on the spur of the moment, decided to slow dance in the midst of the bumping, jiggling, swaying, yelling crowd. Csaba and I stayed glued in our places, afraid to move, keeping as best we could out of harm's way. As things settled down once more and people trickled back to their places, it was getting late and I decided to leave for home with the kids. When I got outside into the fresh air, I was glad to find that after all the noise and a few close brushes with the jubilant choir, I could still hear fairly well and the rest of me was also pretty much intact.

Csaba recounted to me later what happened at the reception. First the pastors were ushered into a small room, ate their meal in relative peace, and left. The others were not as lucky. The guests of honor, who were the bride and groom, their immediate families, and Csaba were supposed to be seated at the table. (The sponsor decided to leave early and did not join them.) The rest of the guests were to eat standing up. However, all the bride's many extended relations from her village decided they were the guests of honor too and sat down first, leaving the true honorables standing on the sides. Since Csaba had been pulled away for the pictures, he came into the dining room late. When he got there, someone steered him toward the table amidst the bustling crowd and shoved him toward a chair. But before he was able to sit down, the current occupant had to be shooed from the chair by the usher. There were stations of food in the courtyard and everyone was swarming around them like bees, pushing, shoving and grabbing. Those who were aggressive were able to eat and took advantage of this by taking large portions; those who were not aggressive did not eat.

It was again pandemonium, though quite different from the exuberance of the ceremony. When someone wanted to sit down at the table, they grabbed the plate of someone else who had just finished and then snatched some rice from the pot. One of Csaba's friends, who was with him at the table, had his spoon taken away from him before he was finished and had to ask for it back. In all the confusion, the guests of honor at the table were not all served due to the hordes swarming around the pot. The servers had been pushed aside. Alexis kept passing his plate on to other people who did not have one, and asking a frazzled server for another plate, only to pass it on again. He hardly ate. To crown the meal, Csaba and several others got food poisoning because the food had been out most of the day while everyone was waiting for the sponsor to arrive. In a tropical climate, a few hours can make the difference between comfort and agony after a meal.

But the couple was married at last, the very first Bakwé Christians to do so. They were married and I trust God will use them as an example to others of what a Christian union should be. May they show the world how a man and wife can love, honor, and respect each other. May they create a small but true picture of the relationship of Christ and his Church.

The people in this culture have a long way to go before they are able to view man and wife as being united in more than just the physical sense, before they see that true honor, respect, and loving care are the backbone of a strong union. It will require some strong marriages to reveal just how wonderful married life can be. In a society where marriages are so fragile that no one wants to pay the dowry up front anymore, may this be an example of a marriage "till death do them part." Alexis and Marie have a hard road ahead of them, one that will inevitably go against the current of their culture. But once the momentum builds and this society turns to Christ, we hope to see all of life, and not just marriages, transformed.

18

Christmas

There is little in our village to signify we are even in the Christmas season. There are no shops specializing in Christmas presents, no lights, no holiday music, no snow or even any chance of it. The market carries a few more products than usual, but the food is still the same as it is all year round, except that some years there are precious few goats left after Ramadan. But what we lack in goats we make up for in chickens. If there is anything that pictures the holiday spirit and Christmas cheer in Africa, it is a chicken. What can I say? Chickens are just the perfect holiday gift. They are not too big or too little. They take almost no assembly and are easily carried tied together and slung over a bicycle. I have seen them in crates up on the roofs of buses with their heads sticking out, wattles flapping in the breeze, or swinging gaily upside down in the hand of a gift-giver walking happily off to another village. I really cannot say enough about chickens. They even look good gift-wrapped, if one has the inclination. Noai once put bows and bells with a touch of glitter on a chicken, and it did have a nice effect until the chicken took off at a run and left bows strewn all over the yard. But this should not deter anyone from trying this wonderful gift idea. They are *the* item to give to friends and relatives alike. They represent friendship and feasting, bonhomie and good cheer. Of course children tend to like toys and candy better—but we all know they are just not civilized yet.

We as a family do have our own Christmas customs here, and even though Noai might like it, I don't give my kids live chickens for presents—we have enough noise and confusion already. We do put up the traditional Christmas tree. This consists of a tropical "pine-like-thing" that I bought once in Abidjan and which sits potted in the courtyard most of the year. Every Christmas it is brought into the house three feet taller. As I write this, it has become so tall it touches our mat ceiling. I don't think we will be able to get it inside next Christmas; we will have to plant it outside and decorate it there.

When we decorate the tree, we take out from storage the usual ornaments and odds and ends, but one particularly memorable year there was something new. Since we had just gotten electricity, Csaba bought us some Christmas tree lights in Abidjan. We all were excited to hang them up—it would be the first time ever in our village that we could enjoy beautiful lights on our "pine-like-thing." The children helped Csaba put them up, and we held our breath as he finally plugged them in. Csaba and I gasped in dismay. These were no ordinary lights. Our Christmas disco lights flashed on and off, each dizzyingly independent of the others, lighting the room with swirling dots that danced on the walls, cement floor and hammock. In the dark the whole room swam sickeningly with a retro strobe effect. The kids, of course, loved it.

One of our family's special traditions is a Hungarian custom passed down on Csaba's side of the family. We wrap up little candies in tissue paper and tinfoil, fray the tissue paper on the ends, attach a bright ribbon between two candies, and then sling the pair onto the tree. When we are finished it looks like the tree has a thousand snow flakes drifting all around the branches. Noai added another personal touch. On the lower part of the tree, she put warbler, sun bird and weaver bird nests that had been abandoned on our property, tucking them lovingly in amongst the green foliage. She had watched their chicks hatch, grow, and leave, and she wanted a remembrance of them. They gave the tree a wild look amidst the blinking lights and snowy flakes.

The wild look lasted only until the warbler nest was attacked by our savage tom cat and destroyed. The other nests were then removed to prevent further aggravation by the cat. The top ornament of our tree was endangered by the parrot, which has an obsession for pretty, bright things—the tree would have to be watched if it was to last until Christmas day. For a final touch, Csaba wanted to add something that represented life here in Africa, so he hung a flyswatter on a branch. We needed more to complete the effect, but since there was only one available, and that one was still in use, we had to take it down again.

To all the Christians in the village, Christmas is the celebration of our Savior's birth and his subsequent saving of the world, and to remember this we rejoice, feast, and give gifts. Each of the two churches in the village has its own customs. On Christmas Eve, members of the Harrist church light candles at midnight and walk around the village, blessing it with their rattles. We hear them do it again at four o'clock in the morning. Our Baptist church, in true African Christian style, stays up all night singing and praying; we hear them off and on throughout the night too.

We have our own special time of singing and reading of scripture. After that we try to get some sleep. This past year Csaba was supposed to preach the next day at the Baptist church, and he wanted to be coherent when he did so. Csaba explained to our team he didn't like these all-nighters because it makes everyone tired and cranky the next day, and incapable of work the day after that for those who choose not to take their vacation then. It happens every year.

For the rest of our village Christmas means something quite different on a practical and cultural level. Amidst the season's steamy heat and sunny skies, it is for them a season of feasting, revelry, drunkenness, and noise. It starts around eight o'clock in the evening and continues all through the night. Most of the people in the area, who are not in church dancing and singing, seem to be in a state of perpetual intoxication. It is a night of noise and confusion. I hate noise and confusion, whether it's from disoriented roosters who have no sense of time or from the tipsy village revelers who have no sense of the volume or quality. On Christmas Eve everyone wishes to share music and gaiety with all their near and distant neighbors. They turn the volume of their stereos up high enough to ensure that *everyone* is having a good time. Since everyone lives so close together and everyone does their partying outdoors, you can imagine the din. The village becomes one big noisy family.

This would not be so bad if they chose to play Christmas carols or hymns at high volume, but alas, they do not—the genre of choice is the modern African "high life" music. There is only one way to avoid it and that is to play something more to your particular taste at a higher volume. So on Christmas Eve last year I played Pachelbel's *Canon in D* at full blast. Hans came into the living room laughing and said, "Oh, that'll show them, Mom!" On Christmas day we played Handel's *Messiah* rather loudly as well since the same music was still going down in the village. The *Messiah* is not bad at that volume but it does lack a certain finesse. One doesn't have the option of not listening to music here at Christmas; it is only a matter of what music it will be.

To survive through Christmas Eve night we closed our wooden shutters, turned off Pachelbel, turned on the fan to drown out the noise, and added earplugs for the final touch. We then were able to get a fitful night's rest. We were finally sleeping well in the early morning when a group of Harrist ladies with their rattles came by at four-thirty to wish us "joy of the season" and ask for a gift. We happily ignored them in our beds. Then we received a call on our newly-acquired cell phone at six o'clock, probably from another well-wisher, and we conveniently ignored that too. Since we couldn't continue to ignore forever, especially since the kids were now up and about, we got up and exchanged gifts quickly before any more visitors came by. Sure enough, by seven a steady stream of well-wishers had begun to arrive. We left the kids to play with their toys while we greeted all those who evidently never went to bed last night.

In the afternoon we were to go to the church where Csaba was scheduled to preach a message before we sat down to a Christmas feast of chicken and rice. With a good night's rest, he was fit for the occasion (he can sleep through anything). The only question was whether anyone else would be fit to listen. When we got to the church early in the afternoon, most of the men and children of the small congregation were already there; the women were still cooking. Alexis was also missing. One glance around the room showed us that everyone lacked their usual luster. So much for holiday cheer—they all looked as if they'd had a long night. Some were sitting on chairs by the walls, staring listlessly into space. Others were prostrate on the benches, trying to catch a few winks. Hardly anyone was talking. We tried to carry on conversations but it was useless with people who had spent the night singing, praying, and dancing.

Firmin, our literacy worker, was still overseeing the details of the festive preparations. Large pots were set in the corner of the church and bottles of coke were stacked in ice. When the women arrived with the rest of the food and everything was ready, Alexis walked in with a group of the village young people behind him. They looked like they'd had rough nights too; most of them were hung-over and a few still seemed drunk. They all were carrying plates and spoons with them in anticipation of Christmas dinner. Then another group of women came in, women who had never seen the inside of our church before, and who could well benefit from the gift that God gives to all who will receive his Son—forgiveness and redemption, life and peace, happiness and joy, the gift they lacked and needed so badly.

After the women sat down, some old men followed with their plates and spoons, and lastly, as if an afterthought, came the most feared and powerful man in the village. I never thought I would see the day that *he* would be inside a church and I am sure he didn't either, but he was promised a Christmas dinner if he did. The thought of chicken must have lured him in.

We learned later Alexis had gone around the village telling people to come and eat, one and all, because the food was ready. The food was indeed ready but he had conveniently failed to tell them a sermon would precede the eating. I'm not sure if I agree with Alexis's methods of bringing in the heathen by failure to mention the fine print, but they came and were waiting to eat. Another minor detail Alexis had forgotten was the necessity of telling Csaba what he was planning to do. Because of this, Csaba had to rearrange at the last moment a sermon meant for Christians to one meant for evangelism. After everyone was seated, Csaba rose to preach using Alexis as his interpreter. He preached on the meaning of Christmas in the true sense and on what would happen to those who rejected God's gift of his Son, Jesus Christ—a joyful and sobering message.

Then the feasting began. Everyone's plate was filled with rice, chicken, and vegetables scattered about in oil—if you want to cook African, you do it with plenty of oil. The guests were also given the customary cokes. If the chicken is the number one symbol of bonhomie here, coke, the universal drink, is certainly number two. The people were happy, their bellies were full, and they had been given something to think about. Alexis and Firmin's tired and pregnant wives were serving the group. I could see the weariness in their eyes. They had worked hard to put on this feast and it had been a success. But they were glad when it was over. Now they could sleep.

The next day Csaba went to work and his workers, who had decided not to extend their vacation time, were supposed to be at work too.

When Csaba went to their courtyards to visit them, they were groggy and a bit touchy. They needed sleep badly.

Another Christmas had come and gone. There is still much work to be done in this little corner of the world amongst the Bakwé people before Christmas will truly take on its intended meaning in the hearts and lives of the people.

19

Handling Disputes the Bakwé Way

When we first arrived among the Bakwé, we entered a culture barely studied before. There was very little in the available literature that even began to describe how these people thought and lived. They were an empty chapter in a book. We are still writing that chapter as we watch and observe and gather information to understand why these people do what they do. And what more interesting and more culturally universal source of information is there than the study of human conflict?

The Bakwé are typically a very—how can I say this delicately?—*lively* group of people when it comes to differences of opinion. Their arguments can become quite heated. In fact, I was told this is why the villages are fairly small: if one faction is offended, they pack up and leave, taking their families with them to start a new village. Since the Bakwé are such forceful people in their disputes, there are certain safeguards, handed down from the distant past, to keep situations from totally erupting and people coming to blows. Different clans would never dream of going to war against each other today, but the two major safeguards are still in place: the third party and the "token" old man. Both serve their purposes well.

The third party is a good diffuser. In a formal argument, the aggrieved side will sit together and make their accusations against the other (rather indignant) party. Both are huddled opposite each other and both are usually fuming. The third party will go to one side and listen to what they have to say. This side will stand up and tell him all their grievances in a manner as loud and animated as the strength of their feelings demands. All of their energy is directed at the third party as if he were the villain himself. Then this scapegoat villain, after patiently waiting for the oration to finish, will walk over to the other party and calmly recount the message conveyed to him. After this is done he will wait for their response. Then the poor fellow will receive the same yelling treatment from the second group as they recount all their frustrations and anger against the other side. The middleman will then walk again back to the other side to repeat, in a gentle and patient tone, all that was said. This will go on for the duration of the argument. Since the two sides do not talk directly to each other, they cannot come to blows. If anyone is in danger of being hit, it is the unfortunate middleman who represents both sides.

The token old man is also a very important figure. One needs to have authority behind one's arguments, and there is great power behind the oldest and wisest man of the village. If he agrees with one side then nothing more can be said. However, I have called him "token" for a reason—the old man is often a bit "out of it" during the argument.

We once had the privilege of witnessing one of these intense Bakwé disagreements. There was a ritual family trial after two brothers had allegedly died of sorcery and poisoning. As usual, Csaba was there in the thick of it finding out all he could about the customs and practices of the people. It turned out to be a fascinating gold mine of information.

The relatives of the brothers from their mother's side came from their village to air their grievances and find out who was at fault, and our village received them. When another village visits in this way, all formal rituals are in place. They had the token old man sitting in his recliner chair off to the side and they had the middleman ready to be yelled at from both sides. It is really a psychological game as each party calculates how they will answer at each turn of the debate.

The token old man quickly fell fast asleep in his wooden recliner chair. He is often asleep when called on to judge these disputes but it matters little to anyone. They just need the power of his name. When our village was discussing grievances they would say, "Old man Badju says we were . . ." or "Old man Badju says he doesn't want . . ." and then they have to wake him up to agree. At one point the other village really laid into old man Badju for not taking proper care of the deceased persons before they died. Poor old Badju woke up just in time to hear the angry words coming his way. Knowing full well what to do when this happens, he shot up in his recliner chair and spouted off at them on a totally unrelated topic. Our villagers had to quickly quiet him down and let him go back to sleep so that they could continue saying, "Old man Badju says. . . ."

In particularly important arguments up to three middlemen are used, meaning each argument and rebuttal must be retold a total of four times before it reaches the other side. The young people sometimes say, "This is ridiculous; we're hearing the same thing over and over!" But it is actually necessary because the long interval of hearing an increasingly calmer version of everything said allows both sides to cool down sufficiently before replying.

If for some reason the safeguards break down and one side becomes too emotional, they will call for the village war cry and use it to vent their emotions. Csaba once asked what would happen if they did not work something out to the satisfaction of both sides. He was told in the past it would have meant war, but now it means relations between the factions would be completely severed and there would be no intermarrying or giving any help or aid to the other side—a very ugly situation indeed.

20

"Cultural Event"

There are many situations in which the wrong answer can do a lot of damage. For instance, we were once invited to be guests of honor at a "cultural event" for the village's young people. There would be "traditional dancing" (they said), accompanied by "traditional music" (they said). We decided to go since we tend to like traditional *anything*. Once we arrived and were shown to our seats of honor, we became quickly aware the young ladies were not dressed in traditional dress but in very tight jeans and tops that did not cover nearly enough. Thankfully Hans was at home that evening.

As everyone was waiting for the perpetually late mayor, the girls began to perform previews of their routines. When I saw them go into action with a kind of slow and seductive dancing, I was shocked and amazed at some of the rotations their bodies were capable of. It was not appropriate for public viewing and we whispered to our wide-eyed kids, "Eyes on the ground." If this was the preview, we did not want to remain for the real thing. Somehow we had to find a way out of being the guests of honor without offending them. It had taken so long for them to accept us, and now that they had we did not want to lose them over a side issue. These things would change later after their hearts changed first in accordance with God's word.

Csaba whispered to me, "This is the world of the young people we want to reach for Christ. This is their new culture which they are trying to copy from the West. See what we're up against?" I nodded my head.

Csaba then got up and told the man in charge we were tired and were not going to wait any longer for the mayor to show up, since it was getting late. The man in charge was upset and said, "Wait, let us honor you first. You can't go now! Wait until we honor you and then take your family back. You can return after that." Csaba could not refuse because he had no reason (that they could understand) why we could not stay a minute longer.

So the emcee got up and spoke about the Bakwé work, and how proud they were of us. We knew they really were trying to please us and did not understand the ramifications of all that was going on. But the real shock came when they called Csaba up to the front, and the emcee said, "Now that you are here, what do you think of all this?" Csaba had to think fast. He could not lie and he could not tell what was really on his heart or he would alienate all those he was trying to reach. They, being non-Christians, were not ready to hear about things like modesty and decency. So Csaba smiled and said, "Yes, I am happy to say that tonight I can now see what this all means." He gave a big smile and everyone was happy.

We left after that, with the official urging Csaba to hurry back, which Csaba said he would if he was not too tired. But of course his wife felt that he *was* too tired, and that was that.

21

Translation

Sitting in the office house, sweating in the dense, humid air as the fan drones constantly in the background— is where you will find Csaba and his men day by day, line by line, word by word, translating the Bible into the Bakwé language.

One day the men were translating Mark 12:18–23, the Sadducees' question about the seven brothers who die in succession, leaving their wife for the next brother until she had married them all and died herself, childless. When Alexis asked for an explanation of the Old Testament custom behind the question, Csaba told him the Mosaic Law had allowed for the brother of a man who died childless to take his brother's wife and to have children by her who would be counted as the dead brother's and, therefore, continue his line. Alexis was troubled and exclaimed, "That is impossible. We can't translate that! The Bakwé would consider that sorcery. We have a custom that will allow a brother to marry his deceased brother's wife, but all the children are then his. If they are to be his deceased brother's children, then somehow that deceased brother must have the power to mystically come back out of the spirit world and claim his children. That is too weird."

Csaba said, "Listen, it's not our custom either, but at least your custom is closer to the way things were done back then, in that it is expected of you to marry your brother's wife. But you also have a custom letting a son marry his deceased father's youngest wife, who would be closest to his age. That is an abomination in the Bible. I didn't make up the customs—we just have to accept them the way they are."

Alexis repeated that the Bakwé would totally misinterpret it. Csaba pointed out that passages like this would have to be explained by pastors and teachers who are taught to interpret the Bible, since no one can change what the Bible says.

It was a hard one. Alexis rubbed his chin thoughtfully. "This translation business really makes you think till it hurts."

22

A Memorable Review Session

Light filtered into the dingy schoolroom, made its way around the many bodies packed tightly in front of the windows, and rested in a dim pool at the feet of Alexis, our translator. He stood motionless at the front of the room, waiting for the right moment to begin the reading. He looked up briefly at those who came to listen and saw the chief with his weathered face and worn hands sitting in the most prominent seat, while the rest of the honored old men sat off to the side with their hands resting motionless in their laps as if in judgment over a new village trial. Then Alexis' eyes reached beyond them to the crowded walls in the back, all the nameless dark bodies, all eager to hear the newly translated text awaiting their approval.

The time was right; he now began: "*Ba po nyakli -o!*" (Lend me your ears). The room hushed; all eyes watched as he looked down to his rough draft of the Gospel of Mark translated, for the first time, into Bakwé. He boomed out in his trademark rich, tonal tenor, "Hear what God says in the Gospel of Mark." He then began reading Mark 2:1–12.

As he read, the audience awoke as if from a dream and started to interact with him in customary Bakwé fashion, the fashion of all people who are truly listening. Interjections came from all corners of the room; first a grunt from the front, which is the equivalent of a hearty "Amen," then an "Awee!" from the back, a true Bakwé lament. As Alexis read on and on from God's Word, the crowd gave a continuous low murmur of approval, of shock, and of delight. They were all engaged with the reading, becoming a part of each scene as they added their comments or exclamations. When Alexis finished, all was silent again except for one sentence spoken somewhere from the heart: "Man, God's word is so sweet!"

As Alexis walked off his self-appointed stage, old men, young men, and children all surrounded him, each asking for a copy of Mark. They *had* to have a copy of that book. Alexis apologized, "It's not finished yet—you must wait." "No, we don't want to wait. Give us that book!" Alexis tried to explain that it was only a rough draft of stapled papers and it would be better for them to wait. Give us a little more time and it would be published. But the old men were not to be denied since Alexis was comparatively young, and in the end he had to give in. Slowly one rough draft went into the weathered hands of the chief, and then another draft went to one elder, and another, until all our copies were gone. Alexis smiled as he got back in the car with Csaba and said, "Well, we'll just have to print some more."

Part IV
Animals

Animals have their own personalities, habits, and funny quirks. They are a part of the intricate world God has created for His glory. Since we live on a farm of sorts, we have lots of animals, and these wonderful creatures have provided us with much of our entertainment. Living in an African village is not an easy life and having these animals around us has made this harsh life seem a little softer, a bit more seasoned with humor and wonder.

23

Mongooses and the Pond

God must have an extreme sense of humor to have created the mongoose. They have the body of an otter, the dark fur of a muskrat, the face and long nose of an opossum, the paws of a raccoon, and the trouble-making capacity of a whole troop of mischievous monkeys. But despite—or perhaps because of—all the scrapes I have seen them get in and out of, the mongoose remains one of my favorite village pets.

I like to take my mongoose, Goose, out in the yard for a romp. This activity is not without its problems, since she can be difficult to catch when she wants to be, and she tends to wander where she shouldn't (mongooses are notorious for doing *anything* they shouldn't). It has happened more than once in an unguarded moment that Goose will find herself on the egg shelf in a pool of newly scrambled eggs, or giving herself a new coat of ashes by scratching in the soot of the mud oven. She was only one mongoose—when we added another, we naturally doubled the total mischief.

To solve the problem of wandering mongooses, I devised a plan to let them out and still keep them in my general vicinity. I made a halter for each one and attached a thin rope connecting the two halters together, leaving only two feet of rope between them. I thought this arrangement would work out well because, not only were they incapable of separating, they were also more easily led behind me. If I wanted to go somewhere, I had only to grab the middle of the rope and pull. This technique worked well in theory, but in reality it proved less practical since mongooses are very stubborn animals. The kids could always tell which direction I had gone by the skid marks left in the soft dirt.

One day I wanted to take our pets out for a romp, but since I had a hard time convincing them of the direction we were to go, I finally had to drag them to the hammocks by the pond and leave them on the grass beside me. They would not go very far since they were tied together and were never coordinated enough to go in the same direction at the same time. Every difference of opinion between the two usually became tug of war between my fat mongoose, Goose, and Noai's thinner Squeaky. Goose, being the heftier of the two, would typically win and drag Squeaky around to the spots she wanted to visit. Squeaky would pull back in vain but the end result would be only a few growls and nips. At least they never got very far out of my sight.

The system worked fairly well until we decided to give them a ride on the kids' raft. One of the little quirks common to mongooses is that they hate water. Noai thought we could help them overcome their phobia with a pleasant ride on the bamboo raft with her. I was skeptical but willing to try. Noai sat down on the raft, but knowing the mongoose's predisposition for escape, she moved the raft a few feet from shore to make retreat impossible. I stepped into the pond to hand her the mongooses as they clung to me in terror, letting out a few grunts and whistles— a mongoose's sign of displeasure.

As Goose passed over the water to the raft, she was doing some quick calculations in her little furry head regarding the distance to the safety of shore. Once she was safely in Noai's lap, I pried the second panic-stricken mongoose off my arm, plopped her in the same place, and turned to go back to my hammock.

At this moment Goose decided she had had enough of this raft nonsense and tried to make her escape. With a lightning-fast spring, she shot off her prison and somehow managed to reach to the pond's edge without a bath, which was quite a feat for such a fat mongoose. Her companion was not as lucky. When Goose jumped, Squeaky was still tied to her, and the result was something like a motorboat taking off before the water skier is ready. With no warning, and no choice in the matter, Squeaky left the raft in a terrific whirl and took a forced bath. Meanwhile, her fat friend was already straining desperately on the banks of the pond, wondering what the setback was to further progress. When Squeaky finally surfaced for air at the pond's edge, she shot out of the water like a bullet and started to put as much distance as possible between her and that hated pond. The two mongooses were finally of one mind and dashed off towards home, whistling and grunting nervously as they went. I laughed as I saw them go—one fat one and one very wet, thin one—and their complaining whistles grew fainter in the distance.

They may not have overcome their fear of water, but they *had* finally decided to work together, at the same time, in the same direction, and with the same mind.

24

Barnyard Chatter

We were eating a meal together when, for some reason, an irate hen started to cackle. She probably wanted to lay an egg and someone was in her nesting spot again. It can be very disturbing to a hen when someone is in her spot, so she continued to voice her disgust loudly in the direction of the nesting box. This commotion attracted our main cock to the scene to perform his duty as Lord Protector; obviously something was afoot and he wanted to remedy the situation by adding to the din with his "cock alarm" noises. Then our female guinea fowl, who follows the cock around as an alter-wife, chimed in with her outer-space machine gun cackling. This in turn started the turkey gobbling. Turkeys cannot stand noise, but they always make it worse by gobbling at it. We tried vainly to carry on a decent conversation at the table with the barnyard in an uproar right outside the window. Finally I went out and chased them all away. Only the turkey continued his racket, gobbling on the run.

We love to keep chickens and other fowl. But if you want to raise these types of birds you must first determine whether the pros outweigh the cons for you. Sometimes I am not sure the benefits actually outweigh disturbed peace and interrupted sleep. The bright, moonlit nights are the worst. Our cocks go through periods of insecurity at night, usually during a full moon. When they have one of these insecurity attacks, they have to remind themselves and the world whose hens those are and who is currently guarding them. I could care less who is on guard in the barnyard, but they tell me anyway: "It's three o'clock in the morning and all these hens are mine;" "It's four-thirty in the morning and I'm the roughest, toughest dude in the village. . . ." It gets old very quickly, but such is farm life.

To solve our problem, we decided to put the roosters in the henhouse at night to muffle the noise, which worked tolerably well whenever we remembered to do it. I woke up one night at twelve to hear our cock happily crowing up a storm, telling all the village roosters just how great he was. I realized with a groan someone had forgotten to put him in the henhouse. It was a full-moon night, which meant all the village roosters would be partying late, boasting, challenging each other, or just exchanging gossip. This of course would mean our rooster would stay up late responding, so if I wanted any sleep that night I would have to remove him from the party.

I got my flashlight and on my way to the front door began mulling over all the different methods of slitting a rooster's throat. As I walked outside into the moonlit night, my thoughts immediately turned from roosters to cobras. All sorts of shadows loomed around me; this was the time of night the cobras came out. I stole slowly and fearfully to the rooster tree, eyeing all the dark shapes that seemed to come to life as I went past them.

I reached the rooster tree and pulled the old boy down, which was easy since he was so tame. When I held his warm body and he chortled to me (an affectionate sign of recognition), my thoughts turned from cobras and slitting throats to positively warm feelings toward our favorite rooster. What a fine rooster I had. As I stroked him, I told him what an excellent fellow he was. When I had put him in with the hens, I made my way out of the pen with my thoughts again turning to cobras. Every shadow seemed to contain an ominous shape, a slender, writhing stroke of death. I crept through the chicken yard, shaking.

Once I was out of the pen and out of danger, I realized for the first time how beautiful the night was with the moon and everything aglow, such a silent and warm night, serene and peaceful. I praised God for His beauty on this mystical night. As I crawled back into bed, I was no longer thinking of murdering the rooster. I was quite content with the night. It is funny how fickle thoughts are. I think I'll just keep the rooster after all.

25

Goose Knots

I was taking the mongooses out for their routine romp so I tied the usual piece of rope between their halters, but even when I do this it does not guarantee a trouble-free outing. With mongooses you never know what to expect. They really must be watched.

I left them in the cocoa forest, but instead of going back to the house as originally planned, I decided to watch them from the bushes to see what they would do. Left to themselves, the mongooses immediately began to dig for grubs in the soft dirt with their long claws. They have excellent noses and can smell a grub or worm several inches down.

After a time of peaceful grub digging, Squeaky, the thin and wiry one, stopped to look up into the cocoa tree above her. I don't know what she saw up there, but the unknown heights must have looked good to her and she shot up the trunk to explore. Goose, the fatter of the two, was still busily looking for lunch in the ground and hadn't noticed her thin companion had left her side until she felt a sharp jerk on the rope. She looked up and saw Squeaky at the other end of the taut rope, straining to go higher but impeded by Goose's bulk. After surveying the situation, Goose decided there might be something interesting up there for her, too, so she shimmied up the tree in a way that only a fat mongoose can.

Once Squeaky felt the slack on the rope, she was free to continue her ascent and did so with gusto until she finally stopped to rest on a side branch. The rope had become hooked over a knob on the limb. In the meantime, Goose was having second thoughts down below. Climbing the tree was not easy, and she began to think exploring the heights was not as exciting as all those snacks left below in the dirt. She turned around and started to climb down, but only made it halfway down the trunk before the rope ran out of slack. This was a terrible predicament indeed, for she was now upside down, clinging to the tree trunk, with her strength about to give out.

She did the only sensible thing for a fat mongoose—she let go. The result of this maneuver was less than satisfactory since of course she never made it to the ground. With the middle of the rope slung over a knob and Squeaky on the other end, there was no slack to allow the descent, and Goose was now suspended from the tree by her halter, spinning slowly in circles. She did not seem to be in any distress but just hung there calmly with her little furry arms hanging limply by her side and her beady eyes darting left and right. She seemed resigned to remain there for some time, and she might have done so if her companion had not intervened.

Goose's fall, instead throwing Squeaky off balance, actually freed her to move farther up her branch, and she managed to slowly raise Goose up. But she finally found her burden too heavy and decided to come down, head first, under the branch and on the wrong side. She descended until the rope, hooked to the limb above her, went taut. Since she was already upside down she could not retrace her steps. By now she was in an awkward position too, and losing her balance—so she also let go.

When I walked to the tree, the two mongooses were hanging precariously in the air, twirling like little furry ornaments, for all practical purposes stuck there for the day. That is, they *would* have been stuck if I had not untangled all the mongoose knots they had made and plopped them back down on the ground where they belonged.

I knew it would only be a matter of time before they got themselves into another quandary. You never know with mongooses. They really ought to be watched.

26

Flying Hen

Most boys Andreas' age have probably, at one time or another, been seen flying an airplane around the yard making the appropriate airplane sounds. Andreas, not being an average boy, took flying to another level.

One afternoon I saw Andreas holding our docile little red hen, Sweetie, in the "jet fighter position" in front of and above his head. The hen, unperturbed for the moment, just sat there in his hand contemplating her dull and brainless existence. She had not a care in the world except for where to scratch the next grub or how to avoid the obnoxious rooster. All this was about to change. She was about to be plunged into a whirl of sheer excitement or perhaps sheer terror—something which she had, before Andreas, never known.

Placidly looking out at life from her high position, she suddenly noticed the ground was moving underneath her. Soon she realized she had left her position and was zipping through the air at an amazing speed. Andreas was running for all he was worth, still holding onto his chicken, completely caught up in his role as the pilot. The hen's former dull and placid look turned into surprise and consternation bordering on hysteria. She could not explain it—all she knew was that she was in full flight, and at that speed and altitude she decided she had better put out all the necessary equipment to keep her there. With her wings flapping in the breeze, she became for the first time a fully alive and liberated hen.

As they circled from the chicken pen to the office I stood watching the spectacle of flapping hen and running boy, my only hope being that the red jet plane would not release any of those packages a hen is so wont to do when nervous. But soon the excursion came to an end and the plane came in for a perfect landing and was left on the ground. The pilot bounded off to go hunting, chopping, or whatever else took his fancy for the morning—apparently there would be no more flights for the day.

The red jet remained dazed where she had landed. She ruffled her feathers, shook herself off, and went back to her old, dull existence of grubs and roosters, just as if she had never flown and never would again.

27

Snake Hunt

It was six o'clock on a typical Sunday morning—typical, that is, until Noai came up to the house from her morning walk and told us excitedly she had seen a large cobra by the path near the pond. I quickly went into the bedroom and woke Csaba. "Get your shotgun, honey! Quick!" Csaba, still half-asleep, got out of bed and went for his gun. As we dashed down the hall and out the back door, I briefed him that his mission was to kill a large cobra down by the pond. He sighed and began to prepare himself mentally for this new turn of events. He had been planning to spend a quiet morning reviewing his sermon notes before breakfast, but now that would have to wait. Killing snakes was a higher priority.

We got to the pond and sized up the situation. A snake was hidden somewhere in the depths of a large flower bush. I told the children to step back, except Hans who would take his part in the kill with his heavy staff. A shotgun is excellent for maiming a snake so it can't escape or strike, but it often does not kill the snake. You have to hit with a blunt object the small head waving at the end of its long rope-like body. This is not easy to do in the best scenario, and with the snake hidden in the bushes it can be very difficult. Another complicating factor was that Csaba, in his rush for his gun, had left his glasses back at the house. But one must not chafe at lost opportunities. One just has to make do with hidden snakes in hazy focus.

We all knew our roles. The younger kids stepped back while Hans manned his post next to the bush with his large wooden pole. I was on the opposite side (unarmed) to make sure the snake did not escape in my direction. I am not sure what I would have done if the snake had chosen my route to escape, but I tried not to think about it. I sometimes wish snakes did not exist.

I could hear the old dog up at the house barking insanely. He loves snake kills so much that he is an utter nuisance when he takes part. When a snake presents itself he barks like an idiot and then rushes in and grabs the snake's tail, which stops the really effective means of killing a snake, since we don't want to club the old dog to death. I also question the wisdom of his strategy of grabbing the snake's tail, but then again, old dogs are not known for their wisdom. So we leave him tied up at the house.

We stood poised and ready for action. Nothing. The cobra refused to show itself. Since the kids wanted action and Csaba wanted sermon-reviewing, he decided to take action by shooting into the bush at a hazy, snake-like shadow. Again, nothing. There was now a dilemma: was the snake dead? If it was not dead, it still refused to come out, and if it was dead, we would not know it unless we went closer. Since a large cobra has a long striking distance, nobody wanted to chop into the flower bush with a machete to find out the snake's current status. Hans finally started poking in the depths of the bush with a long, thin stick. Nothing. We did not know what to do. Maybe we should let the dog loose to find out; he loves to grab dead snakes and drag them around the yard. But then again, if the snake was alive the dog's love of snake tails would be his death, so we left him safely up at the house.

Hans poked again and this time there was movement, and the snake's head appeared at the base of the bushes. It had finally been disturbed enough by all the poking and shooting to leave the protection of the bush and venture out into the open. As I saw him leaving the bush, I stood worriedly at my post hoping he wouldn't come my way and again wondering what I would do if he did. Csaba shot for a second time and realized it was his last shot. No matter—the snake was now wounded and the rest was up to the clubbers. Hans and Csaba followed the snake into the banana grove and I followed them as a guard. The snake suddenly turned and came directly toward me. I choked down a scream and, to my surprise, actually did something practical. I stomped my feet. The snake, feeling the vibrations, turned back toward Hans, who was now in a good position and started to club the snake with his staff. Csaba then struck like lightning at the snake's head with his machete. This time the snake really was dead, and we congratulated ourselves on the demise of another enemy. After cutting the cobra's head off and throwing it down a pit, we let our barking lunatic out, tail wagging, to drag the corpse around the yard.

28

Stinker

Male mongooses are absolutely disgusting. They have the bad habit of marking their territory over and over again, which would not be *so* bad if it did not produce such an extremely evil odor. A male mongoose will sidle up backwards over some object (for example, your sandal) and then make a slow back and forth movement as if dusting it with his hindquarters. To finish the act, he will leave a pool of foul-smelling liquid and then move on to the next spot. I have more than once put on my sandals to find, to my disgust, they were wet. We also discovered later a male mongoose's territory can encompass more than just inanimate objects.

For this reason alone, "Stinker" stays in his cage. I used to feel sorry for Stinker being cooped up all day, but not for long. Whenever I let him out for a romp he either spent his time marking our shoes and furniture, or we found him fastened onto the screen door halfway up Goose's cage, wagging his tail—a mongoose's communication of intense interest.

We originally received Stinker from another missionary family because the mongoose was ruining their ministry. They had let him run loose, and he had the habit of dashing across the yard to nip the bare toes of the African church members who would come by to visit. Not wanting to be outdone by a mere mongoose, one of the members once wore covered shoes. This did not deter Stinker at all—he climbed up the man's body and bit him on the arm. This action sealed his fate. He might have made a good guard mongoose because at night no one really expects a small brown body to come dashing across the dark yard, low to the ground, to nip one's toes. But since this was not his purpose, he had to go, and so he came to live with us. I hoped to breed him with my female, Goose.

At first we thought he would get on well with Goose but this was not to be. He had far too intense an interest in her, almost to a point of total obsession. He spent his days fastened onto the screen wall that separated their cages, wagging his tail and emitting foul liquids—I can only guess he thought she was his territory. When I let him in with her once, he immediately fastened onto her back and sunk his teeth deep into her hide. The unnerved Goose then sunk her teeth into *his* hide, and the result was a terribly messy fight. We tried again several times until I concluded that Stinker simply did not know how to treat a lady right. I think a few screws were loose somewhere in his little male mongoose mind. And so they lived separate lives in separate cages, growling at each other and competing in the emission of pungent odors.

The positive aspect of Stinker's obsession was that it allowed me to take him out for romps without fearing he would wander away and foul the furniture and shoes. If I made sure Goose was with me when we took our walks, I could be confident he would be close at my heels. One day I took them out, Goose in my arms and Stinker following on the ground, looking up at the bundle of feminine mongoose that he considered his territory. No doubt he wanted to sink his teeth into her and perform his disgusting christening routine. I could see his beady eyes calculating the distance between the ground and his object. Without warning he took a jump. He was amazingly accurate for being so low to the ground, but not accurate enough to predict that I would lift her up at the last moment.

After discovering this propensity to jump for her, I began to have more fun with it, putting it to greater use with each successive romp. On one such outing I dangled Goose over some flower bushes, taunting Stinker to come get her. He couldn't resist. He calculated the distance and took a fantastic leap into the air, only to meet with empty space. I then had the privilege of watching him arc back downwards like a little brown comet and disappear into the flower bushes below. This failure did not deter him and he came right back to my side looking up to see if she was still there.

Another time I tempted Stinker to climb a shrub in the yard by holding Goose out at the end of a branch. Stinker dutifully climbed toward her but the branches kept getting thinner and thinner. Undaunted, he went on until he swung upside down under a thin branch. It was only at this moment his intense one-track thought broke and he became concerned with his precarious position. Being unable to right himself in such an awkward stance, he was forced to crawl back down the branch on the underside, clinging for dear life. Stinker must not think much about his dear life, since he was at it again only a few seconds later.

One of the funniest episodes occurred when I noticed our worker washing clothes while I was walking the mongooses. The thought struck me immediately: "I wonder if Stinker would be so stupid as to. . . ." True to form, Stinker took a flying leap and disappeared into the tub of soapy water. He came out sputtering but much cleaner then I had seen him in a long time. Thinking this great fun, the kids and I took Goose down to the pond with "lover boy" close behind. Stinker seemed to be totally unaware there was a pond, since his attentions were so wrapped up in Her Highness, who was perched rather casually on my arm. Goose seemed mildly amused by the proceedings. She would look down nonchalantly at Stinker and occasionally give him a bored, half-hearted growl.

To test our theory of mongoose male denseness, we held her over the pond. Stinker immediately jumped and landed squarely in the pond. For the first time, he seemed to have a rather shocked expression on his face as he swam to shore. He didn't know what hit him. He finally discovered there was a pond and that he was now in it. It was probably his first real swim and I thought it would be his last. Surely he had learned his lesson from the dip in the pond. But since I was not quite sure how dense he was, I decided to complete my experiment with one more trial. I held Goose out again over the water and Stinker went up like a shot and down for another dip, arcing over the water and disappearing into its murky depths. He surfaced spluttering again and swam back to shore looking so woebegone that I was going to pick him up and cuddle him right then and there. But my attention was momentarily diverted to something the kids wanted to show me in the grass away from the shore. As I was looking over at whatever it was, I felt a soft rubbing on my foot. Instinctively I jerked, fearing some horrible creature had crawled onto me. I looked down and saw Stinker sidling up backwards to my foot, rubbing himself back and forth while giving me one of his foul chris-tenings. I am sure it was in revenge, too.

Still there was something intensely satisfying in seeing an aggressive, male chauvinist mongoose suffer the consequences of his attitude. I think he finally learned his lesson because I have not been able to get him to go in the pond since, but sometimes I still wonder whether his brain is wired right. Goose would never act so ridiculously, now would she? We're thinking of letting Stinker go in the forest to catch his own grubs, because he isn't working out as a breeder. Maybe he just needs a few more dips in the pond.

29

Choir of Clucking Hens

It is beneficial for the people in our churches back home to know just how missionaries spend their free time; it's the best way to find out whether they are balanced or not. Some missionaries live an unbalanced life from overwork, never taking breaks to refresh and entertain themselves. This is not the case with us.

Your average person back home has many options for spending their spare time, such as playing golf or going to the movies. Due to our living situation here in the village, we neither play golf nor go to movies. Golf might not be a bad idea if we could make some clubs and use our excess limes as balls. With a little effort we could probably build an excellent obstacle course in our back yard. But jungle golf has remained only a dream, and we have to turn to other forms of amusement.

So one day, in our spare time, we took up the art and challenge of teaching music to a disgruntled choir of singing chickens. The idea of a chicken choir is nothing new, I'm sure. Somewhere in antiquity someone must have thought to assemble a batch of chickens for a musical performance. It really is a plausible idea, somewhat akin to a bell choir but of a much cruder nature.

We found there are many inherent problems in the endeavor to transform a flock of chickens into a troupe of musical wonders, the first and foremost being the problem of catching them. This was soon overcome through bribery. To catch the potential talent we lured them into an enclosed area with rice and then, when they were happily eating, the children picked them up and tapped them on the back to ascertain their voice quality and natural pitch. Thus we were able to audition our unsuspecting contestants for the choir.

As soon as the kids chose their chickens from the motley crew, the finalists were brought to the carport. We sounded them out to determine which were to be bass, soprano, tenor, and alto. We made sure to set them on a perch in the correct order or the wrong note would be sounded at the wrong time. We eventually decided to do away with the cock as bass because not only did the old boy have a relatively high voice, he also refused to cluck on command. This left us with a few crusty old hens beginning to complain bitterly at the inconvenience. They wanted to follow their Prince Charming and go scratch for grubs. We tried to restrain them, but eventually we let them go to follow their leader. After all, a disgruntled choir is simply unworkable. The whole idea would have been scrapped if someone had not suddenly thought of "The Beggars."

The Beggars are a crowd of teenage chickens who insist on sneaking through the screen door of the back porch every day, looking for handouts. They are easy to catch—I only have to yell out the back door, "Here, kitty kitty kitty" and they come running, hoping to share in the cat's meal. We easily chose from among them a soprano, alto, and tenor. The bass part was hard to fill and eventually went to Sweetie, the little red hen who had been Andreas' former fighter plane. The docile and content Sweetie will do anything for a handout.

Now that the auditions were over, we lined them up according to their parts on an old piece of wood in the chicken pen. For our first piece, we chose "Old MacDonald Had a Farm." Noai would tap in turn the backs of the chickens which were to sing their note, and they would then cluck on command. Since each chicken has a different pitch of voice, if we could tap them in the right order, "Old MacDonald" would theoretically be the result. Periodic "positive reinforcements" of rice would also be given to keep the choir happy and willing to perform.

Our choir was performing surprisingly well until we reached the end of the first stanza, when the tenor took wing and left. After all, with the rice finished, why should he stay? Jeremiah was dispatched to retrieve him with bribes of more rice, and more rounds of grain were given to entreat the others to stay. The next stanza began, and everyone more or less clucked at his or her appointed times. But before the third stanza could start the choir revolted. First the errant tenor left again, and the soprano and alto followed close on his tail feathers. Only the bass, Sweetie, perched there stupidly waiting for another handout. Andreas gave her a pinch of her favorite food then took her off for a flight around the yard.

Though I had lost my choir, the experiment had proved a success. At least we had amused ourselves. Rehearsal would just have to wait for another day.

30

Elusive Crocodile

(by Noai)

This is Noai's account of our one and only crocodile hunt. He was actually a small crocodile, about the size of my nine-year-old son Jeremiah. Scenes like this add excitement to an otherwise routine day. We never know quite what to expect in Africa— that is what makes living here so fun. —L. L.

"Crocodile!" my mom screamed from down at the pond. We ran there as fast as we could to see it. Recently our workers had seen a croc in our pond and we were keeping a watch out for it. Maybe this was it. My mom told us to call the workers. We did and everybody came running looking like an army of farmers ready to fight with their pitchforks and sticks. When they arrived at the scene, the water was calm and no crocodile could be seen. Everybody started poking in the water, disturbing the once beautiful little pond, turning it into a soupy mess. Sure enough there was something there. We saw the unknown thing streaming silently away through the water, parting it like scissors do paper, until it sank down into the muddy depths.

The workers made a net out of bamboo. Taking it in hand, they stepped into the pond with the mud swirling about their legs, dragging the net across. When they neared the opposite end of the pond, the streaming thing got scared and jumped three feet into the air, landing on top of a steep bank. One of our helpers shot up the bank after it and caught it. To our amazement it was the biggest catfish we had ever seen in our pond. We caught eleven more catfish that day, and in the end the hunt of the gnarled tooth croc ended up being the hunt of the giant catfish. But to this day we don't know whether the crocodile is still there in our pond or not.

31

Chicken Obstacle Course

Noai once had the great joy of helping an egg hatch. It had been abandoned by a thoughtless hen that somehow decided waiting around for the last chick to hatch was just too much trouble. So Noai took the egg and hatched it in her warm hand. She watched the chick break the egg and push it apart. She watched it turn from a wet, bald, ugly bird into an adorable little ball of fluff quite intent on making Noai the central object of her affection. The chick refused to let Noai out of her sight. As might have been expected, Noai was agreeable to being adored, and adored in return. The two became inseparable and it was not unusual to watch Noai walk through the living room with a peeping chick dashing behind her, trying to keep up with "mom." She lovingly named the chick Sandra. Sandra was a very good chick as chicks go, but soon Sandra grew up to be a fine, strapping young cock. Life is full of surprises. This did not deter Noai at all from loving "Sandy" just the same.

In the meantime another chick was abandoned, and Hans became a foster father. Hans named his chick Edward and had great hopes the chick would grow up into full cockhood. Yet Edward's destiny was to become a cute little red hen. Hans kept the name of Edward anyway and doted on her just the same. Even after both chickens were grown, they were still quite partial to their particular parents and came running to the old, familiar voice. When Hans called out loudly in the yard, "Edward, Edward, sweet little Edward!" out of nowhere would come a red streak, dashing low to the ground in her hurry to see what delectable food was in store for her.

The relationships did not stop there. With bits of food, Hans trained Edward to climb ladders, make hops in the air, and to jump over objects on command. He was pleased with her progress, and it seemed Edward would do anything for food. Noai was working similar feats with her cock, which was just as greedy. An idea was born and it soon became "the Great Chicken Races" of the village of Touadji II.

We set up various brush hurdles spaced about ten feet apart, of different heights and materials. I then took the chickens from their owners and went to the starting line while Hans and Noai went to the opposite end, ready to call their chickens. As they started to call out, I dropped the chickens and they dashed toward their parents. The result of this first race was rather disappointing since both contestants went around the jumps and ran unhindered all the way to the end to receive their treat. Since this was not consistent with the spirit of the race, we went back to work on the course.

We put a side barrier of brush to deter our feathered contestants from taking the path of least resistance and tried again. When the start sounded, I dropped the racers and again they were out of the gate and dashing towards the first brush jump. They both reached it about the same time and winged over it, flapping furiously. In the meantime Hans and Noai were at the end calling out, "Edward, Edward, sweet little Edward!" or "Sandy, Sandykins—Sandy!" This was all the encouragement the chickens needed to spur them on.

The next obstacle was the log jump. Again the chickens flew over it in grand style, except this time Sandy edged into the lead; Edward had lazily half-stepped on the jump as she flew over it. In the next stretch Edward dispensed with the jump altogether and cheated by darting through a hole in the side barrier, leaving Sandy to continue on alone in the straight and narrow way. Once Edward was unhindered by those ridiculous jumps, she half-dashed, half-flew to the finish line long before Sandy (that good honest bird) could reach it. Hans could not refuse Edward her reward since her brain, being the size of a pea, could not comprehend she had done anything wrong. Still, he gave her a thorough scolding for cheating which she, being satisfied with the rice, completely ignored.

The experiment met with mixed success, and more courses were eventually constructed. From then on we had our weekly entertainment "at the races."

32

Wild Things

One of the special things about being a missionary in tropical Africa is living in an environment with a wide variety of animal and bird species. When one of their young ends up in our care through a mishap or as a gift, we have the privilege of raising them ourselves. There are no laws against the raising of wildlife here; no one in the village seems to care what happens to them.

Well-meaning African friends often bring us young wild birds as gifts, and though we prefer these chicks stay in the wild, once the deed is done we must accept them. If we don't, they become the toys of the village children and played with until they die. Unfortunately, many of the chicks given to us or found injured, do not make it. We are sad for a day but we move on; that's life. Things live and things die, and we see it very acutely here, in much more than just the animals and birds. When the wild young survive, they are a great delight to us.

Once Noai found a fledgling miniature finch by the side of a busy pathway. It was bound to become a child's toy soon if not taken by us. So she took it and fed it, and it soon became a part of our lives. The finch was affectionately (if not innovatively) named "Birdie." Birdie became so comfortable with his new surroundings he made himself at home wherever he was in our house. He singled out Noai and refused to go to sleep unless she held him. This soon became a nightly routine: he would complain when Noai first put him in his box for the night and his pitiful chirps, coming from under a jiggling cloth in the corner of his box, would arouse the maternal instincts of my patient daughter, who would then take the bird out of his box and nestle him on her shoulder under her long hair. There Birdie would sit making contented chirps until he fell sleep. Noai put him lovingly back in his box for the night.

Nighttime was not the only time the finch wanted the comfort of a mother. During the day Birdie absolutely had to have her in his sight. If Noai left a room he would panic and try to follow her. Once I saw Noai dash past me to go on some errand, and just a second later came the frantic little black finch, flying at top speed, trying to catch up to his "mom." Once he reached her he was content and sat on her shoulder preening his feathers. Noai often took the bird outside with her when she played. Birdie had no thought of returning to the wild. Even when Noai threw him in the air he alighted right back on her head.

When we went on furlough another missionary took care of the finch for us, and an unfortunate mishap took him. We considered him a delightful gift while we had him, even if only for a short time.

I too tried my hand at raising baby birds when a pair of doves was given to us, little balls of fluff cowering down at the bottom of their box. They had to be force-fed at first until they overcame their fear of their new surroundings. After that they willingly opened their mouths, making a long "weeeee" sound in their excitement over a meal. But feeding a little mouth with big adult fingers was not easy. I often missed the target and plastered the oatmeal all over the sides of their tiny heads, so often in fact that we started to call them the "oatmeal-heads."

One of the doves survived to adulthood and we set him free. He hung around the yard for a few days, eating the millet I set out for him, then disappeared to find a life of his own. The dove was forgotten until one day much later when I felt something alight on my head. I was startled at first—my mind immediately conjuring an image of a large hairy tarantula—but on closer inspection it was only the little dove, now in full adult plumage, coming back to give his greetings. He was a beauty and I told him so. For the next week, in all his handsome attire, he would hang around our yard and often land on a branch near me or even on my shoulder or head, and I learned not to jump when I felt something land on my hair. Then as all wild things should do, he left for good to make a home of his own.

A brilliant neon-blue kingfisher was one bird we really hoped would survive and go free like the dove. Noai, who is usually given the task of raising these orphans because of her loving patience and attention, took the bird under her care. The bird felt so comfortable with her that at night it would hop over to the little decorative shelf by her bed and settle down. When I went in to say goodnight to her, there was the bird like a brilliant sapphire jewel, nestled down among the delicate tea cups on Noai's shelf, eyes tightly shut. But the bird slowly deteriorated in health and one day it died. We don't know why. Maybe we just didn't know how to care for a kingfisher properly, or perhaps the bird was the plaything of an African child and damaged before it came to us. There were tears shed when Noai's wild jewel was gone, but we had no time for mourning when, soon after, Billus entered our lives.

Billus, a baby hornbill, was found when a tree came down. An African friend of ours picked the bird up off the ground and brought him to us. Hornbills like to make nests in hollow spaces in the giant forest trees, and preferring high places, they rarely come down to the ground. Even when young, Billus was a formidable bird whose huge body towered over our miniature finch. He had a classic, formal look with a black coat in back contrasting with a striking white vest in front. His formal attire was set off by a proud face with a pair of haughty eyes gazing out from between thick, dark eyelashes. His crowning glory, was a disproportion-ately large beak that took up most of his face. The whole effect was an aloofness that suggested he was nobody's fool, almost like an old retired butler who, instead of serving, demands always to be served.

While the "butler" lived with us our lives were not the same. Now that we had Billus (short for "horn billus" and transformed later to "Billy boy"), we had to feed him. Given this task, the kids asked me what his menu was to be and I told them that hornbills are fruit-eaters. So fruit was what he got. This unfortunately did not appeal to "His Grace" and he sat on his perch in stony silence, refusing to eat. We began to worry until Noai decided to try feeding him a grasshopper. With a shriek of delight Billy Boy snapped it up, and from that day on crawling things were on the menu. Later research revealed his particular species of horn-bill is an insectivore and will rarely eat fruit.

Billus soon proved to be a heavy taskmaster, demanding a plentiful supply of insects each day. We could not ignore the haughty fellow. He had ways of eyeing us and making disgruntled noises as we passed, let-ting us know his every desire. But even though he asked rudely, he was most appreciative of the meals he received. When the kids would present him with his favorite food, Billus would always scream with delight, swoop down from his post, and grab a grasshopper out of their hands in one powerful motion. Then, like an experienced connoisseur, he would fly back to his perch and mouth the grasshopper, even flipping it around in the air to savor every bit before it finally disappeared down his long, black throat. If the kids failed to bring tribute but wanted to hold him, he would perch on the hand that was supposed to feed him and start gnawing away at it in frustration. Billus was not to be disappointed with an empty hand.

Soon the hornbill was doing so well we decided it was time to let him go in the yard to catch his own food. He had become a large bird and we were tired of feeding him so many times each day. Once he was let loose we thought our load would lighten. It did not. "Billy boy" would find the kids, swoop to a branch near them in a dignified manner, look down at them with his haughty eyes, almost daring them not to feed him. If they didn't, he would start to complain in a way that only a hornbill can. Since Billus was not the sort of bird to be ignored, the kids would inevitably go in search of more grasshoppers. The hornbill would follow closely behind them, alighting from bush to bush to survey the progress of his dinner.

Even with all this wonderful service for "His Grace," one day he disappeared like all wild things tend to do. It was sad, but that was what we intended all along. Still we would find ourselves looking in the sky and wondering if any of the flocks of hornbills flying high overhead contained Billus. When no hornbill came swooping down demanding to be fed, we assumed he was gone permanently.

A month later he reappeared. Noai was out in the back and noticed a hornbill sitting on a tree near her, staring with familiar eyes. To be so near to humans was uncharacteristic for this wild species, so she called out to the hornbill to see if he would respond. She noticed a second bird stayed farther behind in another tree, too frightened to come closer. After several calls of "Billy boy," the first bird swooped low to another tree, a little closer but not too close. Noai called out his name again, and again the giant bird came to a closer branch, moving in a tightening circle. He stayed for about five minutes while Noai called out all terms of endearment he had known before. Finally he took off with his mate and left our lives for good. Still to this day when a flock of hornbills flies high overhead, Noai will whisper his name and wonder how the proud hornbill is getting on with his new wife.

Though it is difficult to see some of our orphans die, we take delight in the ones that live and we marvel at God's wonderful creatures. Someday the Bakwé will also come to see the value in God's wild creation as something more than food or playthings. It is our hope when Christianity is established in their lives, their worldview will include both awe and responsibility for the environment where God has placed us.

Part V
People

A veteran missionary was once asked, "What is it you love about living in Africa?" She responded simply, "The people." Then she was asked what the hardest thing was about living in Africa. She responded, "The people."

We have found that living among the people, even though frustrating at times, is the only way to know and love them individually. We have learned to appreciate our cultural differences. We have learned to laugh at their humor. We desire to see them learn and grow. We mourn when they die, suffer when they are suffering, and care deeply about all that happens to them in this life and the next.

Here is a look into their world.

33

The Old Harrist Priest and the Locked Book

He was old with weathered hands and a wrinkled face. Yet he was in the Harrist church every Sunday, clothed in white robes with a black sash crossed around his chest. He was their leader but he knew he needed to be led. The French Bible the other pastors in town used was a mystery to him. Its contents held the answers to life, the texts for his sermons, and the explanations to his questions. But the questions had long remained unanswered. He could not read. And because he could not read, he had to preach from the memory of what little teaching he had heard.

When Alexis read the newly translated chapters of Mark in Bakwé to the old Harrist priest, he could not hide his excitement. The book that was locked to him was being opened. He was hearing the words of Scripture in his own beloved language for the first time. He wanted to know more. "You have to teach me how to read!" he exclaimed.

As soon as we organized adult literacy classes, the old Harrist priest was invited to attend. When the first class commenced there were about thirty men and women sitting down at old wooden desks with slates in front of them. And prominent among them was one Harrist priest, sitting proudly in the front with his slate and pencil, ready to learn.

34

Javier and the Eggplant Field

One summer Javier, our cook, planted an eggplant farm. It bore well. Each small green bush was heavy with large, teardrop eggplants. It was a beautiful field, and there were many lovely bushes on the lot that bordered it. But not everyone appreciated the field. One Bakwé woman was jealous of his farm and its success. Yet Javier was very generous in giving her and others his eggplants, and the remainder he would sell. Why would anyone want to harm him? In Bakwé country they say if someone is successful, it is not uncommon for others to do their best to destroy him and bring him back down to their level. Because of this it is difficult for anyone to get ahead.

It happened in the middle of the eggplant season when Javier's plants were bearing the most. A Mr. Charle claimed the land bordering Javier's house and field as his next house site. Since Charle was away at the time, he asked a man named Luc to be in charge of clearing the land for his new house. This was welcome news to Luc since he disliked Javier and his Christianity. He disliked the new church growing in the village. He had been a major obstacle to the church for some time and had tried unsuccessfully to get it removed from the village. Here was his opportunity to strike again. He could clear more than he was supposed to on the perimeter of the lot and "accidentally" destroy most of Javier's field.

He soon discovered he was not alone. When the jealous woman found out Luc was in charge of clearing the land, she suggested clearing more land than was needed. In fact she told him to have the workers completely clear out Javier's eggplant field. Luc must have agreed because the next day he told his workers to clear away everything, including Javier's whole field. Luc expected resistance from Javier. But instead of fighting for his rights, Javier took up a hoe and started to chop down his own eggplants while singing hymns to the Lord. He then took the wilted bushes, stripped them of their eggplants, and made a meal to feed the workers. They asked whose field it was and Javier said it was his. They could say nothing and just looked at him in amazement. How could anyone ruin his own field and do it so joyfully?

I think Luc was waiting for a confrontation with Javier about the field. He knew how to fight well with words, and he would welcome an argument with this powerful Christian. He never expected Javier to destroy his field willingly, and he was certainly not prepared to accept the money Javier gave him later from his eggplant sales. For weeks afterward Luc could not look Javier in the eyes. He was ashamed.

Luc knew how to argue and fight and tear down, but he did not know how to handle love and joy—a joy that no non-Christian could be capable of generating on his own. Soon afterwards Luc began to call Javier "my son," and the most formidable critic of the church became silent. He was silenced by love.

35

A Sketch on Death

I was in the kitchen at night when I heard a faint moan becoming gradually louder until it became a wail. As the wail increased in intensity and was joined by others, I realized it was the death wail. Someone had died and the sound of mourning was coming from our neighbor's courtyard. As the news spread around the village, I could hear the wailing grow from one corner to the next until it encompassed the whole realm of the Bakwé in Toudji II. The eerie sound was moving slowly in our direction like a wave over the land which would eventually break in a rumble in our neighbor's courtyard. The death wail can be the most eerie and dismal sound in the entire world. It is a sound that sinks deep into your soul and makes it want to cry out too.

Hans walked into the kitchen and said, "It sounds like a scene from Dante's *Inferno* out there." He paused. "Who was it?" I told him it was GeGe, our neighbor. GeGe had wanted us to take his young daughter back to the States with us to be educated. He frustrated his wife repeatedly by passing out on the floor in a drunken stupor. We learned later he had stolen her money for drink and had passed out again. When she found him, she decided she'd had enough and left for another village before he awoke. Only this time he never woke up. Eventually she found out what happened, and in one of life's cruel ironies, she would be accused of killing him. She left him and then he died. To some the circumstances seemed obvious. But accusations were for the future; now it was a time of mourning.

The mourning lasted all night. The next day, bright and early, Csaba came into the kitchen and reminded me we needed to make an appearance and greet the family. Greeting the family after a death is very important—if you do not, it tells them you don't care. Greeting is not optional if you want to keep your friends, and though it is so important, I always dread the experience.

As we walked toward our neighbor's house, the sun's rays were slipping sideways over the houses and into the courtyard. I glanced up past the rooftops at the giant trees on the horizon bathed in the day's new light. It was light that warmed the earth, opened up the flowers, and caused the birds to sing as if their throats would burst. Light—a symbol of our life in God. We were walking in this light yet I knew that soon we would be plunged into a kind of hell, a hell we had already seen too many times here.

We sat in the courtyard of the deceased on little wooden benches. Rows of people sat around us on the few rickety stools and chairs or on the ground on a piece of cloth. All was somber and quiet after the last bout of wailing. Most people's eyes were fixed on the patch of dirt directly in front of them. It was very quiet except for the muffled sobs coming from a group of women, the closest relatives of the deceased. Slowly it started again, like a wave building strength. The soft tonal wail was joined by other voices all over the courtyard and then increased with force until the group was impassioned with emotion. Women sobbed uncontrollably and others ran to console them. The men wailed too. Only the children, wide-eyed, looked on in silence. The wave slowly ebbed again and the people became calm, but it would not last long. It never did.

In the relative silence I heard a far-off muffled cry coming from the road and moving toward us. A group had just arrived from another village. As they came closer, more people in other parts of the village joined with them wailing until they had reached a fevered pitch. I could see them making their way in a slow shuffle through a far courtyard. I noticed one woman in front who seemed to be the leader. In her mournful cry she was talking, uttering words of despair, words devoid of hope, words that would bring the dead back to life if they could. The rest of the group echoed her, continuing until she had reached the courtyard. She shrieked, fell to the ground, and began rolling in the dirt, sobbing.

Others ran to comfort her and lifted her up. Then the next wave of wailing rose from the courtyard. After a socially acceptable amount of time, we excused ourselves and returned to the house until the time of the burial.

It was now the late afternoon and we were waiting in the courtyard. They had mourned all night and most of the day, and were now spent: their voices hoarse and their eyes red, finally ready for the deceased to go to his final resting place. The Harrist choir was now there, shaking their rattles in a soft, rhythmic beat. The song began and the choir moved forward in a slow march. We all filed in line behind them as we made our way down the hot, dusty street toward the cemetery. All the while they sang a low chant and their rattles pulsated a numbing beat into our heads. We turned off the road onto a prepared patch of ground on the fringe of the Bakwé cemetery. As everyone filed in around the coffin, we looked past the wooden box to an empty square pit and the red earth in its depths.

All was quiet. It was blazing hot. A prayer was said and the coffin was lowered into the ground. As the clods of red dirt were thrown onto the coffin with a thudding despondency, a family member started screaming. She sank down to the ground sobbing with her hands held out as if she were calling the dead back to life. She was lead away and comforted with little success. As the coffin slowly disappeared, I choked back my own tears as yet another familiar face left this earth to go on to another world, a world with no hope, void of beauty and sunshine. It is always a sober reminder to us of why we are here. We are the messengers of light—God's light. As we labor steadily, this light is shining little by little into the darkness. It is just a matter of time.

We turned off the dirt road and entered our property. I felt drained and tired. As I walked down our gravel road and around to the back yard, I saw the bougainvillea cascading in all directions like a bright pink waterfall, not just one waterfall but many splashing colors all around the borders of our land. As I continued around back I noticed the large, pagoda-like flowers that graced the walk, brilliant red flowers standing there like temples adorned with dazzling blue butterflies. My old dog greeted me with a whimper and a wag of his tail. He looked up at me with his milky blue eyes and muzzle flecked with white hairs, glad I was home. The children came pouring in from the back of the property stampeding past me on their way to some new adventure.

Life is a wonderful gift of God, and because God has given us eternal life through His Son we can joyfully live this life to the fullest. May He grant that gift also to the Bakwé.

36

Josephine

Csaba called out from the living room and asked me to accompany him on a visit to a sick woman. She came to our little church but stopped coming some time ago for her own reasons, which we had never quite figured out.

When we arrived we stood at the door of a little wooden room with a dirt floor. One small window let in a little light. Other patches of light came through the holes in the walls and down by the floor where the wood had rotted away. We were told to enter. Lying on an old, bare mattress covered with a dirty cloth was the once proud and lively figure of Josephine. She was now a shadow of her former self, so thin, pale, tired, and weak that raising herself up to shake our hands took an arduous effort. My heart sank. After Csaba and I greeted her softly, she slumped back down on the mattress where she lay breathing hard in rasps and wheezes as the flies buzzed around her head. Now and then she would lean over and give a weak cough gurgling deep down in her chest. I felt a growing uneasiness. She was in a bad way and I knew it.

I had seen people at this stage before and they rarely make it. It looked like either a bad case of pneumonia left too long untreated or the final stages of tuberculosis. We have seen people die of tuberculosis. It is not an easy way to die. Josephine looked bad, and we did not want to handle this case with only our meager supply of antibiotics. Csaba prayed for her and told her he and his Bakwé team were pitching in money to send her to the hospital. We were to leave for our workshop center in Bouake the next day and would not know the outcome until we returned, but we had little hope of seeing her alive again. All we could do was pray.

On our way back from Bouake three weeks later, we wondered what news we would get upon our arrival. We fully expected Josephine was dead. When we entered the village, a woman came running up to our car. I sat there in total disbelief. There was Josephine, in full health and wearing a big smile. She thrust her strong hand into my own stupefied, limp one, pumped it vigorously, and said, "If it weren't for you all I would have been dead."

"What happened?" I asked dumbly.

She just smiled and said she would tell us later. I reluctantly turned from her as Csaba started rolling the car toward the house. She came by that night to tell us what had happened. After we left, her relatives carried her to a taxi they had rented and took her to the hospital. The doctor gave her a lot of medicine and she faithfully took it. She was scared she would not make it. She was so weak that she did not have the strength to walk or bathe herself.

During this time the village abandoned her. We had seen this disturbing custom before: when someone has been sick and seems to be at the point of death, villagers will visit and tell him to confess what he has done through sorcery to cause harm in the village. In this society, sickness, or any other negative event, is not considered a natural thing. If something bad happens then some*one* must have caused it, and the guilt of such sorcery is thought to fall back on the one who worked it. So if the sick person actually confesses something, he will supposedly recover and the other current ills in the village will be explained. If he will not confess, then the village will abandon him as a sorcerer, and once abandoned, he will often die. Then it will be universally thought he was guilty after all, for an innocent person would surely have gotten better.

That is what happened with Josephine. Being a professing Christian, she had no attempted sorcery to confess. But during her recovery she had much to think about. She thought about the church she had abandoned, and her relationship with God, whom she had also turned her back on. During this time of suffering, when she thought she would see her Maker soon, she turned back to Him. And it showed. Her face was radiant and smiling in the powerful way she had. She told us she was coming back to church because God had taken care of her. It was good to see someone return to the faith they once left. It was a welcome sight to see the living when you had expected to see the dead.

Part VI
Culture

37
The Magic Trick

What is culture? According to one dictionary it is "the beliefs, customs, arts and institutions of a society at a given time." The differences among cultures make entering another culture fascinating. People from a specific society will see things and events through their own cultural glasses tinting their interpretations of life. I have different basic assumptions about life handed down to me by my western, Christian heritage. As we enter another country, we need to learn to observe well and find out what those basic assumptions are and how they influence the people's perceptions of life. Like working on a difficult puzzle, it is fun to fit the pieces together and try to see life through their eyes.

One day our missionary friends from another city stopped by with their kids to visit us. Sam, the husband, knew many magic tricks and gave us a show. Our kids were fascinated by the tricks and eagerly looked on, though they were not the only ones watching—I noticed the worried look of Javier, our cook, in the background peering in. When the show was done and we went out to the back yard, we met Bibionay, our yard worker, and his friend Tesu. Sam showed them the trick of pulling a handkerchief out of an orange. Bibionay and Tesu were utterly stupefied at this marvel. In fact, Tesu was so shocked by what he saw he fell to the ground (which was Tesu's way of saying he was completely flabbergasted).

When Sam saw their anxious reaction, he showed them how it was done and they immediately burst out laughing. They could not believe they had been so easily deceived. They wanted Javier to see it. I went into the kitchen to get him but he would not come, saying he had too much work to do. I could see he was troubled so I said, "He'll show you how it works; please come see it." Reluctantly he came. The trick was done and Javier stood there watching in silence, the very picture of foreboding. But when Sam showed him how it was done, Javier's face lit up and he too roared with laughter.

A basic belief of many Africans is that God is far away and that spirits have real control of the world. These spirits cause all the evil on earth and man is powerless against them, though some men can use the evil power of the spirit world against others for their gain—this is called sorcery. Christians here in Africa have to be constantly reminded God has power over the spirits and He gives total protection to His children. Our workers believe this, but they did not know how to interpret what they saw in Sam's magic show. Instead of looking for a physical explanation they immediately thought Sam had gained occult power. The thought of sleight-of-hand never entered their minds.

Sam told them the sorcerers operate through trickery and deception. He said he could reproduce some of the tricks they do. He told them to be sure not to always trust their eyes, but to look for an alternative explanation and always trust in the all-powerful God, who is the Author of truth and not deception.

38

Mother-in-Law

"It is a good thing you are building a separate house for your in-laws. Now you will not have to look at your mother-in-law's face," said my husband's Bakwé friend. It was true we were building a mud and stick house for an office and guest room, but the purpose was not so we could avoid my mom's face.

The man continued, "How are they going to get here?"

My husband responded that he would be driving them from the city, of course. This was met with a look of shock and horror as the man exclaimed, "Oh! But she will be in the same car as you! And where is she going to eat? Certainly not with you?"

My husband confirmed that of course my mom would be in the same car and eating at the same table with him.

The man replied, "Oh, no! This is not good. You must not eat with her, not live in the same house, and not talk to each other. You must be like a groveling worm in her presence."

He then proceeded to give my husband a few "worm" lessons. I could only imagine how my mom would react if Csaba were to mumble his greetings in a weak, humiliated voice and then proceed the rest of the day to slink around corners and avoid eye contact. It might have quite the opposite effect. My parents might actually think of taking me back!

Not so with the Bakwé. If one does grovel and go to the utmost extreme to avoid his mother-in-law, then there is less chance that she will reclaim her daughter. The explanation of this attitude lies in the way the

Bakwé handle conflict. The Bakwé were historically a volatile people living deep in the forests. Whenever there was a major dispute among them in the past, they would solve the problem by splitting the village and starting a new one somewhere else. The Bakwé had only small villages because they could not keep the peace long enough to form a large one. In modern times, the villages were relocated to the main road so schools could be built in central locations. In our village of Touadji II, several villages were initially grouped together to benefit from the one school. This caused no end of strife and even violent arguments. In one argument a fistfight broke out and required many men to stop it. In another, a woman became so angry she ripped off some of her clothes and started screaming, which is a Bakwé sign of the most extreme indignation and wrath. But the offended party can never leave because they cannot take the school with them.

This pattern is also seen in their marriages. Marital disputes often involve a great flurry of words before the wife finally storms off to her mother's. If there is a problem between a mother-in-law and her son-in-law while she is visiting, she could take her daughter back with her if she is angry enough. Complicating matters even more is the supposed mystical power mothers-in-law possess and might wield if provoked.

Of all the relationships in existence, that of a man to his wife's mother is one of the most volatile, so the best thing is not to give temptation a chance and to stay out of harm's way. An argument cannot happen if you are not there to start it. Just become a worm and nobody gets hurt.

My husband tried to tell the people he had a good relationship with my mother and he did not need to act like a worm in her presence. The Bakwé would laugh nervously and look at him with an expression that could only mean "Well, we'll wait and see." When my parents arrived, we all went into the village to greet the people and to show them how we all got along. Everyone grinned uneasily, though most of them accepted this strange familial serenity with relief, saying this was a much better way of handling things. The incongruity was too drastic for some old women who were quite scandalized by it all. Once we realized this, my husband stopped accompanying us on our visits to the village.

Needless to say, my parents had a wonderful time visiting and no, they did not want to take me back. I just thank God that we do not have to handle conflict the Bakwé way. I am sure Csaba does too.

39

Hospitality

A missionary was relaxing at the table after a meal of rice and sauce with his family and an invited guest. The guest, an African friend, leaned over and said to his host, "You know, I have worked with missionaries in the city for years and you are the only one who has ever invited me in to eat." He said this with a hint of sadness, as if he had received a major rejection from the others. Maybe, through his eyes, he had.

Hospitality is an extremely important concept in a country which believes time spent relating with people is more important than time spent working on things. In a village where everyone knows each other, if you have not invited people to share a meal when the appropriate moments arise, you have shown them your heart is not open to them. You are a closed book in an open society, a society judging closeness by time spent together.

Hospitality in our village can come in many forms, but certain things are always the same. If people come to visit unannounced (which is the majority of the time), you always offer them water. Depending on who they are and from how far away they have come, you can offer them cokes or coffee as well. But you must *never* give them a list of choices.

One day Alexis' sister came to visit, and I offered her a choice of coffee, tea, or hot chocolate. She did not respond but just stood there as if paralyzed. Her mouth moved, trying to say something, her eyes looked around anxiously, and I could imagine her breaking out into a sweat. Alexis quickly came to her rescue, whispering rather loudly, "Just tell her you want chocolate."

She mumbled the word "chocolate" rather weakly and stood there dumbly while I served her.

Later I asked Csaba about this odd behavior and he said, "People in this culture don't often make a lot of choices since their diet is limited. To have a choice is confusing." I agreed as I remembered my first reaction to the supermarket cereal aisle when we came home once on furlough.

"Another thing to consider," Csaba continued, "is when you offer a choice of something, you are communicating that you are unsure of whether you really want to give it or not. You didn't tell them they could have it, you only asked them if they wanted it—there's a difference, you know. What you need to do is tell them there is coffee for them. They will either accept or reject the offer and no extra choice is required."

I tried it next time with positive results. No one in the group went in a state of paralysis when I told them there was coffee waiting for them. But what if they really wanted chocolate?

Sharing meals is very important and has well defined protocols. If some guests are still hanging around as lunchtime approaches, you need to invite them in to eat lunch with you. You never chase anyone away by saying, "Well, I'd better get in to lunch now; talk to you later." If for some reason you do not want them to eat lunch with you, then you do not eat yourself. How can you eat when you have turned your guest away empty? If the husband decides to forego lunch, then his wife and kids may eat without him, out of sight. They do not really matter much in this scheme of things as long as the headman is there to shoot the breeze with the guests. If it is obvious that someone keeps coming around during mealtimes and you wish they would stop, then just serve them foreign things like Jell-O and they will never show up again.

It is different of course in America where everyone knows they are supposed to leave the premises at mealtimes. If someone invites you to stay and eat unplanned, you know what you are to say: a firm "No, thank you." My repeated attempts on furlough to get my American friends to eat unplanned meals with me usually had this same result. They know (culturally) they should not stay because they assume my invitation is (also culturally) insincere. To them I am just being polite—a politeness like a bud which produces no flower. Not so here in Africa. Everything is in full bloom as guests join you readily at every invitation.

As a guest in Ivory Coast, if you are offered food and choose to accept it, you must taste it but you do not have to finish it. No one is going to harass you to finish your food because others are starving in Africa. If you have accepted your host's food then everyone is happy, and the leftovers will go to the children, who eat to the side of the adults, usually on the ground.

Once an old woman came to visit us during mealtime. Csaba called out that we were eating and asked her if she wanted to join us. We did not think she would but she did and entered an environment very foreign to her own. We watched as she shuffled slowly over to our table, laid her cane on the floor, and sat down, looking as if she felt rather out of place. She was used to sitting on a stool by the fire instead of on a chair at a table. We gave her some of our food and she tasted it with hesitation. She did not eat much beyond the biscuit, but she seemed pleased that we had honored her by inviting her in. After an acceptable amount of time and many smiles later, she retrieved her cane, gave a Bakwé blessing, and took her leave by silently shuffling out the door.

Sharing a meal means you care enough about your guests to welcome them into your home, even if it is unplanned. It means you will share what you have with them, even if it is but a little. It is not the amount or even the quality that really matters. It is merely the fact you have invited them in and shown love using the cultural means of doing so. There is something about eating together that builds bridges and opens doors beyond the surface level. For a ministry like ours, it can make the difference between success and failure.

40

Plump Ladies

"My, you're looking good!" said my African friends, with smiles of approval, after our return from furlough. "You're fat!"

What constitutes beauty is not the same the world over. When I came back from furlough, it was true I had gained some weight. Since the Africans are very free with their comments, I was told at once how beautiful I was now that I had finally increased in size. They had only known me to be rather unimpressively thin and were amazed at what wonders my native country could do for me. They announced proudly my mother must have been feeding me well. But as typically happens when we return, I slowly began to lose the weight I gained, and with it I could see the reaction of my admirers change from pleasure to dismay. "What's happening to you? You're losing weight. Oh, no!"

When I had lost a bit more and arrived at my typical African weight, they would say, "We don't understand it. It must be the food. You don't do well on the food here."

Another person added, "It must be because you no longer have your mother to cook for you." I could just hear them all sighing in sympathy.

We were reminded of this different standard when one of the local men was commenting on their "Mrs. Akwaba" (translated "you have arrived") contest. A woman from our village entered the contest and had gone quite far. She was comfortably plump. The man said, "You Americans just fool around with your Miss America pageant. Those aren't the *real* women—there's nothing to them. That's just child's play. Now take our contestants for example: they are a bit older, more mature, larger, in good form. Now that's a woman for you. That's the type of woman we seek for a wife."

This is too true in a place where people can have trouble putting food on the table. To have a little extra on you is a sign of the prosperity everyone seeks to attain. When you have achieved prosperity, you want to show it with your body. Being thin is definitely not "in." Plump is beautiful. This has been a hard thing for some of our larger American missionaries to deal with. Since the Africans are very vocal about appearances, they have met these colleagues and commented directly on their size with much approval. "You're fat! You're looking really good." This is not the ideal way to compliment an American.

Everyone here wants prosperity, which is defined as the capability to eat well and show it. When we were back in America, it struck us how the people had been enjoying prosperity for a long time and were desperately seeking to show less of it, at least on their bodies. Two different worlds, two different ideals—the one where the other wants to be. So the next time you seek to downsize your person, remember you have this problem because you live in a prosperous nation where there is plenty to go around. Most people are not as lucky. Be thankful for what you have when you enjoy all your festivities. So many people are not able to enjoy what our nation has. Thank God for His blessings; We have certainly received a lot of them.

41

Smith's Ghost

When we translate we must be very careful to use the right idioms. Since idioms are (according to Webster) "The way of speaking and putting words together peculiar to a language," we have to know the cultural meaning behind the words and phrases before we use them. If we are not careful, we could be communicating something entirely different from our intended meaning. To illustrate this point, here is a true story of what happened to an African Christian who once came to the States to study.

The African student was assigned to stay with a Christian couple whom I'll call "the Smiths." All was going very well with this arrangement until one day when the student was left alone in the house. That morning the Smiths had decided to go out for a day in town, so they said goodbye to their African guest and left. He was studying very intently at the table when the phone rang. Not wanting to let it go unanswered, he picked it up and said, "Hello?"

A voice on the other end said, "Hello? Is Mr. Smith there, please?"

"No, he just passed away." (His incorrect translation for "he went away.")

"Uh, really?" said the voice incredulously. "I didn't know that. I'm sorry. Is his wife there?"

"No, she passed away with him."

The voice faltered, "Um, I'm sorry to hear that . . . and who are you?"

"I'm his ghost." (He meant to say "guest," but with his heavy accent the diphthong came out just a little bit wrong.)

When the confusion was later explained to the African student, he was very embarrassed. Fortunately no damage was done, and the two gentlemen were able to laugh at the humorous memory. But stories like this remind us of our serious task. It is very important in our translations to see that we use the right words to convey the meaning the Bible intends. We do not want any disillusioned Bakwé Christians—or, for that matter, any embarrassed translators.

42

Revenge of the Market Ladies

Market ladies, that fierce breed of die-hard produce sellers, that perni-cious element of the vendor world—may their lettuce never wilt and their tomatoes never squish, but may they learn to leave us lesser intel-lects alone in their nefarious efforts to sell yet another orange or mango. Masters of their trade, these aggressive and persistent women know their business well. They can pawn off more fruit on unsuspecting and inno-cent victims than anyone else I know. When I visit their booths, I always come back with more fruit than I wanted. It never ceases to amaze me.

It was a hot day with all indications it would get hotter; already the sun was up high in the sky and burning down intensely. The streets were full of people shopping, loitering, and going about their business. We were shopping too, but not in the "usual" way done by most people back home—that is, in grocery stores and malls. We would have to go from shop to shop and from stall to stall to get everything we needed.

We were just beginning our list of places to stop. Csaba decided I should go to the fruit stand first since it was across from a small shop where he needed a few things. He parked the car and went into the shop while I went to the little outdoor wooden stalls holding all varieties of fruit and vegetables. As I approached I was immediately surrounded by a wall of women holding various items in their hands. They had come from other stalls nearby and each wanted to attract me to their stall first.

Just in case I was having trouble seeing all the items at once, the bags were shoved higher towards my face so I would not miss the quality of what was inside. There were oranges and mandarins, bananas and beans. Surely I would want all of these things and more besides. This overt display of merchandise was unnecessary in my opinion, since I could plainly see the fruit in front of me. Who could miss it? Who could escape it? Who would dare ignore it? But market ladies are not known for their subtlety.

"Take these oranges. They come from Morocco," one woman said as she thrust a bag of oranges into my hands. Another chimed in on top of her, "Do you want some mandarins? These are so sugary!" I thanked them both and said "No, not today." I hadn't come for oranges or mandarins—I have five orange trees and three mandarin trees back in the village. I was shopping for mangos and vegetables. I tried to give the bag of oranges back to the woman, but she would not take them back! If I kept them in my hands I would eventually have to pay for them, so I placed them on the ground and began to go. The orange woman quickly scooped them up again.

I pushed my way through the wall of women and finally reached the table I wanted. The woman behind it very happily started to fill my order. As I stood there waiting, my new friends, the orange and mandarin ladies, tried approaching me again with their produce, but this time with louder voices so that I would be sure to hear them.

"Please take some oranges. They are from Morocco!"

"These mandarins are excellent. How many kilos do you want?"

I refused for the second time and tried to ignore them. I was soon to find out how difficult that would prove to be. Since I was not making any obvious moves for my wallet, the mandarin woman cut up a mandarin and shoved it towards my face to prove how wonderful they really were. Obviously, if I only tasted one of her marvels of the fruit kingdom, I would surely buy some. I turned to her just as the mandarin nearly hit me in the face, and the orange lady, not to be outdone by her competitor, opened up one of her oranges too. I was walled in with a dripping orange and a messy mandarin on either side of my face.

"Now, really!" I said, "I don't need oranges today." Then I felt a tug on my skirt. I looked down and there was a little Jula girl with an armful of bananas looking up at me pitifully and asking if I could please buy some. I told her "No, thank you" and quickly turned away to order some avocadoes.

Undaunted and personally insulted, the mandarin lady returned with her next attack. "I just talked to your husband and he said he wanted some mandarins. Five kilos, in fact." I couldn't help but wonder at the sheer audacity of the woman. These ladies never give up.

"Right, I don't think so," I said.

Of course she assumed I was playing hard to get and it would only be a matter of time before I would break. To her it was not a matter of whether I would buy, but how many kilos.

The sun was hot on my head so I tried to move farther under the shade of the stand's big umbrella. I had to sidestep all the fruit laid out on the ground, and also had to maneuver around the women trying to get me to buy their produce first. The lady behind the stall filling my order mentioned to me her mangoes were the best, and why didn't I get some? Mangoes were on my list, so I wearily nodded my assent. I asked for only four mangoes this time as they were quite large.

The mandarin lady now had a pout on her face and she started to whine, "You never buy anything from me. You always buy from the others. You haven't even bought a hundred francs' [fifteen cents] worth! Come on, just a hundred francs' worth?" She seemed as though she might start to cry at any moment; I hadn't realized how deeply I had offended her.

By now I was beginning to feel claustrophobic, surrounded by a sea of hot bodies. I finished giving my order with the last of the vegetables. When I had what I wanted, I walked away toward the car with the lady from the stall carrying my box. We were not alone. I could hear a familiar voice behind me, a constant droning in the background, a monotone which went on and on about Moroccan oranges and wondering what could possibly be wrong with me. They were from Morocco, you know! She obviously had not finished telling me about the virtues of her citrus. After all, I hadn't bought any yet, and that was not only incomphrensible but totally inexcusable.

As this never ending appeal was going on behind me, the lady who filled my order said I owed more than I had given her. I showed her my list of calculations and when I came to the mangos I found that she had put in two extra mangos on the sly and was adamant about charging me for them. I proceeded to extract the unwanted mangoes from my box. Csaba had arrived, and the mandarin lady instantly darted in his way to persuade him his wife had wanted mandarins but had forgotten to buy them.

I went around to the front of the truck to escape. As the mandarin lady was working on my husband at the back of the truck, the orange lady had silently followed me to the front of the truck. She was not to be outdone by her competitor. She stopped me before I got in and proceeded again with her "Ode to an Orange" routine. I was so tired of it all and the sun was so hot. I wished she would just go away and take her oranges with her.

Then I realized I had a way to make her go away that never failed. A few minutes went by and a short conversation ensued. After it was over, I breathed a sigh of relief. At least the orange lady was finally off my back for the day, even if I had finally broken and bought two kilos of oranges, despite my five trees of oranges back in the village. I did not really want oranges. I wanted peace, and peace is bought here at a price. I hoped that Csaba was faring better with the mandarins.

"Hey Lisa, did you really want five kilos of mandarins?"

"No! And make sure there are only four mangoes!"

He gave me a knowing look and shut the back of the truck. I quickly dashed into it for safety and peace while Csaba paid the women. As I settled on the hot seat in the stuffiness of a truck that had sat in the hot sun with the windows rolled up for awhile, several boys came by and hovered around the open window, blocking what little breeze there was left. They tried to the best of their ability to convince me I needed bracelets and table napkins. I told them "No," which was a mistake since it meant that I was interested in them but was playing hard to get. The droning about the virtues of bracelets and table napkins went on and on, so I turned my head the other way and tried to ignore them. Don't they have anything better to do? Can't they see I'm not interested? When they finally left, a healthy little beggar boy came by and started in on me with his pitiful looks and outstretched hand. What was taking Csaba so long? He was probably fighting his way through the irate ladies we hadn't bought anything from.

Csaba, meanwhile, was trying to make it to the truck through the market ladies and at the same time convince a windshield wiper seller his wiper blades were not needed at the moment since our truck had two perfectly good ones. Also, could the wiper man please step aside so he could get into his truck? Csaba finally got in and we drove off down the road and away from the mad fray. Out of the corner of my eye I saw a lone, desperate figure running after us. Who was it this time and what did he want? I was too tired to care. I was just relieved to have left all that noise behind us.

We turned the corner and went down several blocks to a little Lebanese store where we could get some more groceries. As we got out, whom should we see puffing up behind us but the windshield wiper man! He said he'd had quite a time trying to keep up with us in traffic. A guy could hardly run with his arms full of wipers! After catching his breath he proceeded to remind Csaba he had forgotten to buy his wipers. How many pairs did he want? I was not about to stay around for this one, so I went on into the store to get what I needed. Before I disappeared behind the counters of goods in the little store, I looked back outside the window to see how Csaba was faring. I could not believe my eyes. He was actually buying wipers from the man! At least he could not tease me now about buying two kilos of unwanted oranges. He later told me he couldn't help but reward such a valiant effort of running through all that traffic, all for the sake of selling him a pair of windshield wipers.

A few moments later when I left the store, a new market lady, whom I had never seen before, approached me. This was her street and she was holding (horror of all horrors) a bag of oranges up to my face.

"Want to buy some oranges? They're from Morocco, you know."

To be fair to the vendors, they are not all the same. Some parts of town are more aggressive than others, and we usually try to avoid those. We also try to build loyalty with one person who runs a stand, because she will chase all of her competitors away for us.

In Ivory Coast I have noticed all the people who sell the same item congregate in the same area and aggressively compete with each other. I have walked to a certain section of town and been met by no less than eight women selling nothing but peanuts. They all rushed at me at the same time, shoving peanut jars in my hands. Of course, if I try to give the peanuts back they will not take them.

In some markets in Abidjan—notorious for agression— I have been grabbed by the arm and forcibly pulled into a stall. It can be quite frightening if the seller is a man, but the rather large women vendors can also put a powerful (and frustrating) hammerlock on your arm. Once they have you, they are not about to let go until your wallet is emptied for their wares. Csaba has had items thrown into his car as he gets in to leave, and then the vendor will chase after him demanding to be paid for the wares Csaba has "forgotten" to pay for. With much exhausting experience, we have learned which vendor spots are relatively peaceful and which are not.

Market shopping can sometimes be fun if you are up for a challenge—the challenge being to come away with exactly the amount of whatever it is you wanted at the price you wanted. I am usually not up to the challenge. If I can get something in a supermarket (there are a few good ones in the main cities), I will do so, even though the price is higher. I like peace, and peace is bought here at a price.

43

A Trip to Town

It was market day, and we were driving through town. The day was typically hot, and the people were milling about in the shade of the shops. When we arrived at the main market area, we were forced to slow down considerably as the stream of people flowed into a torrent of bodies walking, shouting, loitering, selling, and buying. The bright West African cloth they wore created waves of color on every side.

The paved road was rough and worn down through long and heavy use, leaving potholes of varying depths jolting us constantly as we rolled along. Sometimes the "paved" road faded away entirely until it was only a fancy in our minds; then we were painfully aware when it returned to torment us once again. The streets were wet from yesterday's rain. Our car hit the puddles and sprayed dirty water into a flow of rivulets down the muddy bank leading off to the vendor's shacks below. Sometimes the puddles were so deep the truck left a small wake behind hitting anyone unfortunate enough to get in the way. We dodged vendors, goats, and market women laden with trinkets, plastic kitchen ware, and toiletries carried in tin pans on their heads.

We swerved around taxis, nearly hit other private cars, and finally came to a standstill in a cloud of exhaust from a vehicle of ill repute. As we waited for the road to clear, it was thronged again with the crowds, a kaleidoscope of people coming from nowhere and going to nowhere. No one seemed to notice there were cars on the road, and we wanted to use it. Slowly the path cleared, and we were creeping along again, but I

could see we had another stop ahead. Carts piled high with stacks of wooden boards came rolling onto the road in front of us, apathetic to the possibility a car could hit them. Another cart appeared from the opposite side laden with intricately woven mats, while a small mound of field grass with legs ambled by in the direction of the goats.

Navigating through all these obstacles, Csaba pulled off the road, parked the car, and walked toward an open-fronted store where there were men leaning against the walls—passing the time of day, doing nothing and wanting nothing. He greeted them and went inside, walking past huge bags of flour, sugar and rice on the floor with big metal scoops in them ready for measuring. When he reached the front counter, the owner met him and started to fill his order by taking items from the small rows of shelves lining the back wall. These shelves reached the ceiling and were sectioned off into compartments containing all one could want: soap, tea, coffee, noodles, sugar cubes, oil, shampoo, a few plastic toys, and other basics. The countertop was just as cluttered as the shelves with razors, pens, stacks of papers, a tin of lollipops and a big lazy cat with sleepy eyes half open, flicking its tail aimlessly. As Csaba waited, a slight breeze blew into the shop and with it came the acrid odor of the street— smells of rotting vegetables, stale water, and the masses of sweating bodies in the humid air outside.

After this stop we were once more outside and creeping along on the road. I noticed a tangle of about thirty wires dangling from one pole to another above one wooden shack. These wires seemed wound and tangled in every direction, eventually reaching shacks and shops where tiny light bulbs hung from the ceilings by a single wire. In one of these shacks a tailor was hard at work on his treadle sewing machine.

We inched forward into the food market. There was produce of all kinds—homegrown onions, long-stemmed green avocados, deep purple eggplant, stacks of freshly picked okra, basins of fresh oranges, bright yellow papaya with its shiny black seeds inside, bananas of many sizes, and vegetables of every kind. These were all spread out in a gallant array on wooden tables or on plastic sheets on the ground. One table held nothing but various spices, filling the air with their pungent sweet aroma. There were tables holding only smoked fish brought in from the coast. On other tables, slabs of raw meat sat peppered with flies. The sound of the trade language, Jula, could be heard all around as people surrounded the different areas and haggled for a good price.

We bartered for a few items and left. It was taking us forever to make progress in the car. I glanced out the window and saw we were now in the "fast food" section of the market. Slices of plantain bananas sizzled in oil as a little girl surveyed their progress. Her neighbor sold small yellow cakes stashed in bags. A man had meat roasting on sticks over a fire. A girl was paring off the outer rind of an orange to cut off its top and sell it as orange juice on the run. A large Jula woman lazily stood watch over bread, intended for sandwiches, lying in neat piles on a bright tablecloth amidst a cloud of buzzing flies. The flies in the market are everywhere and inescapable. Puffs of them rose and fell from the dirt as people walked by. Csaba stopped in the road and flagged down a girl with bananas on her head. He bought a few for us to enjoy as we headed on down the road.

Everywhere vendors were selling and calling, their voices mingling with the sounds of the street: honks of car horns, calls for passengers, children yelling, babies crying and people chatting. Through all the noise a radio blared African "high life" music. A bus was parked partly on the gravel shoulder of the main road but could not be bothered to get totally out of the way. Suitcases, grinding mortars, fresh vegetables, pineapples, yams, a few chickens, and even a goat were tied up on its roof, waiting for the trip north. We stopped at a small bakery to pick up some French bread. Each piece of bread would need to be passed through a flame on our stove at home to sanitize it from fly-borne diseases.

We turned down a dirt side road and were relieved to be out of the crowd. As the car pitched and rumbled along on the heavily varied surface, we passed house after house and scene after scene: children playing in the streets, men hanging out and talking under trees, women doing laundry or pounding yams in rhythm—everywhere there was movement. The walls of the houses were made of boards slapped together, or patted-down mud, or cinder blocks, and most were covered with zinc roofs in various stages of rust. I saw a church in the middle of it all, looking very much like a small boat in a sea of houses billowing up the hills and over the horizon in unending waves of zinc roofs.

We gradually made our way out of the town, back to our village and property with its welcoming cool green grass and refreshing shade trees around the house and no other people—for the moment—but ourselves.

44

A Visit from the States

Bakwé children played in the cool shade by a mud kitchen, women were washing up dishes in a metal basin on the ground, and a few chickens pecked in the dirt as a goat ambled by. In the village it was business as usual. Under a spreading tree, a group of older men sat in a circle on old stools and chairs, some with African cloths wrapped around their torsos and others in trousers. Most of them had gray hair, a badge of respect and authority. They were all staring at one man and talking excitedly among themselves in their tonal language, occasionally making guttural expressions of surprise and delight. Our church in Idaho sent us a husband and wife team, Roy and Bev, to encourage us. We greatly enjoyed our visit with them. What I found fascinating was not so much the reactions of this couple to Africa, but of Africa to this couple. Everything about Roy, his height, size and his gray hairs totally wowed the community. He caused quite a stir.

Opposite the older men, sitting also on rickety chairs, were Csaba and I, our children, and Roy and Bev. It was a normal village meeting, except all dark eyes were glued admiringly on Roy.

As they stared at him with unabashed amazement and approval, one man finally blurted out that Roy had arrived—he was their ideal of a man. With that declaration the meeting began and Csaba introduced Roy and Bev to the village elders, who gave Roy the honorable Bakwé name of "TuTu." They stood for a few minutes just nodding and smiling at him. Csaba finally broke their reverie and asked if they could please give a name to his wife Bev.

Their attention briefly and reluctantly left the grand TuTu and shifted towards the more diminutive Bev. They could only give the equivalent of a long "Hmmmmm." Since the names they give define the characteristics of the person, they had to determine what about her was nameable. They looked at her long and hard but nothing stood out; they talked back and forth but no name would come. She was of average African size. They could not think of a name for so unimpressive a figure, and in the end she just had to remain nameless. (We later gave her a Bakwé name ourselves.) She, like I, would have her status and position in her husband—she was respected because she was the wife of the honorable TuTu.

We left the meeting courtyard and proceeded to the next one, as it is the custom to introduce newcomers to the whole village. I was looking forward to seeing how the villagers would react to Roy, and I was not disappointed. We came into the neighboring courtyard and Csaba greeted the people in Bakwé. They responded with the appropriate smiles and Bakwé response. I was next in line to give my greeting, followed by my children. We all shook each person's hand, called out their name, and said "Ayo." Each person responded with the same greeting. Then Roy came in to greet them. I watched as their faces lit up in total, unconcealed awe followed by exclamations of incredulity that America could produce such worthy men.

It must be nice to be so admired as TuTu was. But not everyone reacted in such a positive vein—in one courtyard a child screamed and fled. Another old woman, after greeting Csaba, took one look at Roy and buried her face in her hands. She stayed this way for a minute until she started to laugh at her own rudeness and slowly raised her head. As she tried again to greet Roy, she broke out into a half-suppressed giggle and squeaked, "Oh, Saro [Csaba's Bakwé name], he's so scary!" This was followed by more muffled snickers as her eyes closed in laughter and her shoulders gently shook at the hilarity of it all.

The grand TuTu would be a hard act to follow.

Part VII
Trials

45

Thorns and Roses

God continues to give and give to us. We find pleasure in all He gives us and it is wonderful. It is wonderful to have life and have God filling every corner of it. We are learning that happiness and enjoyment in life do not depend upon one's current situation. Even in hard trials that make us suffer and groan, if we look beyond ourselves we will see the roses, fragrant and sweet in the midst of the thorns. In the end, when we look back over our lives, it is the roses of God's faithfulness that we will remember the most, and not the thorns of our trials.

The thorns for us are the constant moves from place to place and the desire to be stable in our own home. Yet the roses are all the unexpected gifts and pleasures that come our way from having made yet another trip. The thorns are the wrenching pain of having to say goodbye to another close friend. Yet the roses are all the wonderful times spent with those people and the memories they have left with us. Thorns are sickness; roses are God's comfort. Thorns are the deaths of loved ones; roses are the closeness that comes when God wraps His arms around us and fills the space they left. Thorns are hardship; roses are laughter. Thorns are the fears that come from being in dangerous situations in the field; the roses are God's reminders in His word of how He will care for us and never let us go. As the years go by somehow God swallows up all the thorns in life and leaves only the sweet smelling fragrance of His hand in control of all things.

Though life is not always easy for us, we feel we are living in a place surrounded and supported with blessings. This does not mean the absence of trials, but the faithfulness of God in them and all the added kindnesses He gives us every day—just because we are His children.

46

Opening the Floodgates

"Watch and pray, lest you enter into temptation. The spirit indeed is willing, but the flesh is weak" (Mark 14:38). The unexpected: when we need God's grace the most. When we are ready and prepared for an inconvenience and when we are feeling physically strong, we can handle anything with an amazing presence of mind. It is when a surprise comes and we are at the end of our resources the temptation comes to complain or become discouraged. When we are at the end of our resources, God is at the beginning of His?

It was moving time again, a time of last minute details and packing. We had to be up in Bouaké for our conference the coming week and there was always a never ending list of things needing to be done before we left. This time it was going to be harder because I was not feeling well. I did not feel positively ill; I just had no strength or stamina. I felt tired after only a little work. We were to leave for Bouaké on Monday morning, and since I had been schooling the children all week, the packing was left for the coming Saturday.

On Friday Csaba decided to take me to the doctors in San Pédro to see why I could not get my strength back. I had just gone through two months of a lingering sinus infection, and though I had gotten over it I was suffering from fatigue again. The doctor told me I was anemic and put me on iron for the next three months. The iron would not start to make a difference for a while so it would not help me with the energy I needed to pack on Saturday. But if I packed in short bursts and rested often, I might be able to get it done in time, and the kids would be helping me. Csaba had his own list of things to do on Saturday, such as going into town to withdraw some money for the trip, talk to his workers about their jobs for the time he was gone, and settling their finances. He might not have time for everything. On top of this, I mentioned to him that I needed help with packing. He understood.

That night, when we came back from San Pédro, I had very little strength left from the day's activities. As we ate our dinner, Javier came in and mentioned to Csaba that his pastor was ready to do the baptism at our fishpond. Csaba had known about this—someone from the church had asked him just two days before if they could use our pond to baptize a new member of the large Burkinabé church Javier attends. Csaba had asked the delegate to send an elder or the pastor so he could discuss just what this would involve and what was required of us. Then we could talk about "when" it would take place. The church has over four hundred members and having them all over would involve a lot of preparation. Csaba told Javier he was still waiting for the pastor to arrive here to talk, and he could not make a decision until then.

Javier shifted a little nervously and said, "Uh, they are all coming tomorrow in the morning to have the baptism." We all looked at him stunned.

"Tomorrow?" Csaba said incredulously. "I never gave my consent to this. We are supposed to pack tomorrow. I can't have them all over here. We don't have the time or energy to receive them."

Javier said nothing. What could he say? After he left, a long conversation ensued at the table as we all gave our opinions on the matter. My plea was the most passionate of all since I knew what having all those people over would involve. As the hostess of the house, I knew I did not have the emotional or physical resources to do it at that time.

Csaba felt he needed to be out among the people during the ceremony. It was not only expected of him socially; he also had to protect our property from mishaps. We had enough experience with crowd behavior in Africa to know when many people congregate in the same area, minor damage could result. This was just par for the course—the normal hazard for the hospitable here in Africa. The children were especially concerned about their intricate little clay cities they had constructed all over the back yard which could easily be crushed.

There were numerous other preparations we would need to make, such as roping off the deep end of the pond—at the last baptism the pastor fell backwards into the deep end with the newly baptized clinging desperately to his shoulders, and many Africans do not know how to swim. Then of course there would be people asking me for drinks and possibly coming into the kitchen, which would all take time—time we did not have to spare. I again made a very impassioned plea to stop the event. They could use the river like they'd always done in the past. This church was not even in our sphere of ministry—why here?

It is never an easy choice. We must choose carefully which extra ministry activities we take on, or we could eventually be worn down to ineffectiveness in the specific ministry God has called us to. A village is not an easy place to live at the best of times because you live right in the middle of your work. At the worst of times it can be intolerable. Unless our time is carefully managed, life in the village can quickly run out of control. There is always a constant stream of requests for us to do this or that, and though we like to help out, giving in to each new request is like opening the floodgates—inevitably more similar ones will follow, perhaps on an even grander scale. There is a fine line between when we should decline and when we should let ourselves be stretched once again.

Csaba sat at the table thinking for a while and said, "I'm really in a quandary. I don't want them to come tomorrow, either. It will be too much in an overloaded schedule. But I can't turn them back at the gate or we could damage our relationship with a church here past repair. They wouldn't understand at all. You just don't turn people back at the last minute. It is not African. [Of course it's not American to impose four hundred people on someone without sufficient notice and without waiting for the person's consent either!] If only the pastor had come beforehand, then we could have talked about it and set another time, but he didn't."

"Don't they know this is inconveniencing us by showing up almost unannounced?" I said.

"They don't even consider if it would inconvenience us or not. They would think, 'Of course they would want to have us for a baptism. It would be a great honor for the missionary to have us, and it would bring him much prestige.' They don't seem to understand the concept of running on a tight schedule like we do. Time doesn't have the same meaning here. People and relationships are far more important to them, and all work and obligations are expected to be dropped for the sake of the relationship. We'll just ask for God's grace, and I'll take time out of my morning to oversee it. We have to remember a baptism is a happy event, a joyful occasion." It certainly didn't seem so at the time.

Saturday arrived and the pastor came at an early hour to our house. As we suspected, it was too late to turn things around since the location of the baptism had already been announced to his congregation. He said there would be about a hundred people coming, which was a great relief after we expected four hundred. I was first busy around the yard making sure the workers raked the leaves and completed other preparations, while Csaba was desperately trying to get in a last meeting with his translators before the floodgates opened. I finished with the outdoor preparations for receiving the people and then went inside to pack, but I was running out of steam. I slowly put the trunks out and spread the piles of clothes the kids would put in them.

Soon I slumped down by the trunks in a crumpled heap, teary-eyed, which was how Csaba found me a few minutes later.

"What's the matter?"

I gave the classic response: "I don't know." (Translated, "Everything in general and nothing in particular.")

"Are you sick?"

"No, I've just run out of steam, and I have so much left to do and we still have the baptism coming."

"Just stay in the house. You don't have to come out. If I show up that will be good enough for them. Go and rest, and we'll just leave a day later. I'll work it out somehow."

So I went to bed and Csaba tried to snatch a few more minutes to go over the schedule for the next week with his Bakwé colleagues.

Soon the church members started to arrive, first a trickle and then in gushes like a happy rushing stream bubbling over with excitement. They filed past the office in long lines where Csaba shook hands and greeted each one. Then one hundred excited people went down to the pond with Csaba following. They were going to baptize forty new believers. As they made a circle around the pond, the kids stationed themselves off to the side to make sure no unsuspecting feet accidentally trampled on a miniature clay city.

As the service began, one hundred people rang out with joyful voices, singing "I have decided to follow Jesus" and other songs. Then one by one the new members were lowered into the murky depths of our pond and came back up to be received with joy into the church. After this, the baptized women, all dripping wet from the grand occasion, went into our guesthouse to change clothes, as the men filed past to change at Javier's house. Javier was very busy in the meantime getting drinks for those who asked. After that, the masses flowed up from the pond all chattering and in high spirits and went into our front yard to consecrate this memorable occasion for all time by taking photos of the newly baptized by the flower bushes. Then one hundred happy people thanked Csaba profusely for his generosity and left as they had come, first a rushing stream, then a trickle, and then silence. As I lay in bed I thought, "May God bless them!"

Remembering this, I am glad we could be a part of this happy occasion by opening our home. I was at the end of my resources, but God was not at the end of His. Though we do not seek to stretch ourselves beyond our perceived capacity, it often just happens, and when it does, grace and strength come from above and somehow it always turns out right.

This baptism had been for the Burkinabé church, but we long for the day when it will be one hundred Bakwé people attending a baptism in our pond. May God open up the floodgates of His mercy and salvation to the Bakwé as well.

47

Typhoid

I had fallen dangerously ill. We were in the village waiting for my parents to arrive with Eryn, a teenager from our church who was coming to live with us and help us out for a few weeks. Just before they were scheduled to come, I came down with a bad case of bronchitis that turned into the first stages of pneumonia. While I was in this weakened state I was exposed to typhoid and subsequently contracted it.

At first we did not know why I was not fully recovering from the pneumonia. I started to feel better after taking the course of antibiotics, but then I unexpectedly took a dive for the worse. There were no other symptoms during this time except extreme fatigue, a fatigue so deep it felt like I was helpless in a car careening out of control, heading for a crash. We sought the Lord in prayer as to what to do and He answered us every time with specific guidance. Because of His answers, we knew when to seek help outside the village in San Pédro. From San Pédro, we knew when to leave for Abidjan and how to arrange for the whole family to get there using our one car. Every step of the way He guided us and helped us by answering those prayers. We never felt alone.

I remember a particularly vivid moment in San Pédro, when we were getting ready to make the trip down to Abidjan. I was lying in bed and suddenly felt myself going under fast. It was the strangest sensation I have ever felt. Eryn, who was helping us by packing my things, kept looking over at me anxiously. As I was lying there I felt the Lord say to me, "I could take you now."

I remember responding, "Yes, you could take me. But who will take care of Csaba and the children?"

I felt Him respond back, "I will take care of them."

Then I had peace. I knew He would.

At the same time, as Csaba was looking at me worriedly he felt God say to him, "I could take her now." Csaba realized that God very well could take me and he struggled with it as well. It was not easy for him, but finally he yielded me up to the Lord to do with as He saw fit. Then he had peace.

The next day we traveled the six hours to Abidjan, and the same day I saw the doctor. She performed every test she knew and still could not diagnose my illness. She said there were two others in the hospital with the same symptoms and she did not know what to do with them either. It was a mystery. Since I was not technically ill, the only thing I could do was to return home to rest. My parents and Eryn stayed for a week or two more before they had to leave. Their presence during this difficult time gave me much needed encouragement and help—God sent them just when I needed them most.

A week later the doctor called and said the two others in the hospital had been diagnosed with typhoid. I went back to the hospital and tested positive. It had been difficult to diagnose the typhoid because we were all vaccinated against it and the usual symptoms and tests did not apply to us. She also warned me the treatment for typhoid could make me deathly ill. Because of this she would try to mitigate the effects by building up the dosage gradually.

After I started the treatment, I took another dive for the worse. The doctor, highly concerned, suggested I be admitted into the hospital for surveillance. I spent a few nights there hooked up to an IV and began to feel much better. I had a room to myself and it was lonely in the mornings when nobody but the nurse and a few doctors stopped by to check on me.

The afternoons were different. I was so glad when Csaba and the kids came to visit me. The first time they came was especially interesting since the kids had never seen a hospital room before. As Csaba settled in a big chair by the bed and started to chat with me, I noticed the Venetian blinds flapping up and down and in and out right behind Csaba. When I asked Hans (then 13) what he thought he was doing by flailing the blinds around so wildly, he merely responded that he was trying to figure out how they worked. He soon tired of this and went with Andreas to explore the bathroom and all of its interesting and unfamiliar gadgets. Jeremiah just sat on my bed and started kissing my arm, giving it all the attention it had lacked since I had come to the hospital. He had been worried about me, and it was reassuring to him there was still an arm there to kiss. Noai sat opposite and began patting my other arm.

The boys soon returned, and as I continued to talk with Csaba I noticed a pair of legs sticking out from under my bed. I looked down and asked what he was doing under there. A muffled voice responded, "I'm trying to figure out how this thing works. I think I got it figured out now . . . just a minute . . . okay, Andreas, crank her up!" I slowly felt myself rising. "That's enough . . . crank her down now!" For the next few minutes I went slowly up and down until Hans came out and announced triumphantly how the bed worked. They made me laugh until they turned to "figure out" the IV system and I suggested they leave *that* alone.

Csaba announced it was time to go, and everyone filed out, waving their goodbyes. Then there was silence, silence and loneliness so deep it cut down to my very soul. When you are used to a happy bustling household of children, being without them is a strange experience. To have life is to have the noise, motion, laughter, and cheer of children. The silence and loneliness was like a weight wrapped around me pushing me down, crushing me. During this time I cried out to God. I was determined to return to my family soon.

The next day a friend from our church back home, who had come to Ivory Coast on business, accompanied Csaba and the children to the hospital to visit me. It was so encouraging to see not only my family, but also someone from back home. Then a few colleagues from our mission stopped by as well. To have a visit with those that cared meant so much to me. On that day, I began to feel slightly better. The next day I went home.

There was still a long, hard recovery ahead, but the scary part was over. It looked like God would let me stay on this old earth a little longer, and I was thankful. I was still very weak and the recovery would be slow. The first month after I came back to our center in Abidjan from the hospital, I was mostly down in bed or on the couch. I could not walk far, and Csaba had to carry me up the stairs of the hallway if I wanted to watch a video. Friends and colleagues continued to visit me in the apartment and even made us meals. Slowly I started to get better. Alexis came down to Abidjan to see how I was doing and said the Bakwé villagers were all worried about me.

The first day I ventured outside for a very short walk, Alexis was greatly relieved and told Csaba he knew now that I would get better. When I regained enough strength to walk a fair distance on my own, we went back to the village. I was still very fatigued and rested often. Sometimes I wondered if I would ever recover completely or if I would have chronic fatigue for the rest of my life. During this time I rested in the Lord, prayed, read, and slowly started to take on more of the housework. Four months later, I woke up one morning and noticed for the first time I was not really tired anymore. I knew I had pulled back into the low range of normal fatigue. It would not be until a year afterwards, when we went home on furlough, that I would pull out of it completely.

During my sickness I learned so many things—things that will stay with me for a lifetime. The major part of the sickness had lasted about six weeks with a five to six month recovery period and then another year to regain my full strength. The people who helped us during that time, or visited, or wrote, will be forever etched in my mind. I will not forget their kindness and neither will God. It was like a glass of cold water given to someone in the extremity of thirst. There are times when people give and it's only a nice thing and quickly forgotten, and then there are times when people give and it moves a mountain in your life. When you give to someone truly in need, the results are magnified a thousand times.

48

Letter to a Missionary Friend

I wrote this letter to a missionary who contracted typhoid during the time when there was an epidemic of it in the country. Many missionaries contracted it. Some were affected for only a month, but others felt the effects for years.

Dear Karol,

We have been thinking about you, praying for you and hurting with you through all this. Hang in there. I pray you will recover your strength quickly. Some people recover quickly, but are you prepared for it to take a while? It could. I found that the faith to go through the scary part of the trial and the faith to go through the long recovery are two separate things to be learned, and you need to be prepared. In some ways I think the second part is the harder of the two.

Let me explain. When we went through the scary part (which was the part of running around to doctors, going in and out of the hospital, and wondering what the end would be), we found we were carried by God through the support of the church, our family, and friends. There was an urgency then and nothing else mattered except survival. Life for us stopped and focused on that one thing. But when I started getting better and was no longer in danger, the focus from my support system changed off of me and onto other things.

Life slowly went on. To find life going on as usual and yet not being able to be fully a part of it was like the hands of my watch had stopped while the other clocks in my family ticked on. It was like being left on a dock and watching the ship I was supposed to be on chugging without me back to sea. I was in life but not a part of it. I no longer had any usefulness. It was a frustrating feeling, wondering when or if I would fully recover, and if I didn't, what would my purpose be? I found it more difficult during these times to be patient and have faith. It takes a different type of outlook.

I love being busy and I find a day successful if I have accomplished much for the Lord. I feel the Lord is happy when I have gotten through my list for Him. But that is not the best outlook. To judge success by accomplishments can be a dim enterprise when God limits your ability to do them. What I have learned is that the foremost accomplishment to focus on is bringing Him glory by enjoying God forever; with that will come the fruits of the Holy Spirit, which are love, joy, peace, patience, kindness, goodness, faithfulness, gentleness, and self-control. We can have all these things when we cannot actively do anything, and we can fully please the Lord in this alone. When the circumstances allow for us to do more, our "doing" will flow naturally out of our "being" in Him. We can't control our circumstances but we can control how we respond in these circumstances, and God will be pleased with that. Our purpose is to be content with what He gives us and to truly enjoy Him forever.

Another pitfall easy to fall into is letting yourself worry about the 'what ifs' such as, 'What if I don't recover?' or 'What if it takes longer than I thought?' I find it helpful to remember even if the worst thing happens, God is still there directing and controlling, and the car is not without a driver, the ship not without a helmsman. Let Him take you where He wills and see what blessings He has in store for you. I have always found Him faithful in everything, and so will you. I have learned the most when I have gone through the severest trials. I couldn't have learned those things any other way. There is always a blessing in every trial. Look for it. It may not come in the way you expect it, but it will come.

I know this is hard, yet God has His purposes and His designs, and we need to have our will be so obedient to His that we will follow Him anywhere—even into seeming disuse.

49

Out of Sync
(Trials of a Peculiar Nature)

It is furlough time—that time of laughs and suppressed giggles at the missionaries' expense as they try in vain to adjust to their native culture as if they had never left. The two cultures are so different and the adaptation is never easy. Aside from the usual— standing stupefied in a grocery store among overwhelming choices, adding oil to the frying pan when cooking hamburger, greeting every last person we pass on the street, or shifting all our groceries to the left hand to pay with the right ("clean") hand— we are really just average Americans. A collection of some of our more memorable adjustments follows. Since my teenagers supposedly no longer make any blunders, I am restricted to telling stories only on myself or on the kids when they were younger. Despite this limitation, these stories still provide a brief glimpse into the average symptoms of a missionary-come-home.

When our kids were all young, they were enthralled with the new life on furlough and all the wonderful things in it. The day after we arrived back from Africa, Andreas (then five) discovered of all things a mask, snorkel, and pair of fins in his grandma's toy box. What fun, what magic! He had been told about all the neat things in America, and now here was a sample for his very own use. He put them on and went outside in his shorts to find the coveted tricycle. I woke at some early hour on a cold, fifty-degree morning, after many weary hours in flight the day before, and looked out the window to see a little boy pedaling furiously past in shorts, mask, snorkel, and fins. Was that really my son, or was it some momentary apparition blown in from Africa?

Another fascinating object was the toaster. We can only get French bread in Ivory Coast, and since that does not fit very well into the average toaster, we have never had one in the village. But Grandma did, and I woke up another morning to find all three children huddled around the toaster, putting piece after piece of toast in and watching it pop back up. Whenever a piece popped up they would all exclaim to each other in delight and then put in a new piece. They must have gone through the whole bag of bread before the excitement died down for the morning. We had toast for breakfast that day and many days after.

But the toaster could not hold a candle to the garbage truck. When it was garbage day, the kids would dash out the door and follow the truck all the way down the street, watching every move the men made. How exciting it was to watch the garbage just disappear in that huge metal mouth! Back in the village, garbage is just pitched out of the way without much ceremony, and what fun is that? (It is none too hygienic either.)

On furlough we rediscover the wonders of modern technology. The first week we were back, Grandpa took three of the kids and me to the grocery store. When we got out of the store and were walking towards the car, the trunk suddenly flew open and the kids said in amazement, "Grandpa! Your trunk just opened all by itself!" Grandpa just smiled and put the groceries in. After he showed them how the remote opener worked, they could hardly wait to try the trick again. I found the trunk opener very handy. I am not one given to remembering things, and once at a garage sale I needed to find my sister's car but couldn't. I stared in dismay at a row of similar-looking cars, having completely forgotten which one was ours. Then an idea struck me. I took out the remote opener, pushed a button, and sure enough, one trunk flew open.

This gave us the idea to do an experiment on the car as we waited for her to finish with the garage sale—we wanted to find out just how far away we could be from the car and still be able to open the trunk. Someone manned the controls and walked down the sidewalk pushing the button at short intervals, while the others would shut the trunk each time it opened. To the passersby it must have seemed our car had the hiccoughs and my son was trying to remedy them. This went on until we found the limit of the range two houses away. It was a most exciting time for all of us.

It is not just the technology here that can surprise us—nature can too. One day on a family walk through a meadow in the country, my son discovered in the grass a flattish pancake-like object made up of dried, all-natural materials. These wonders of the grasslands are what my father calls "cow pies." Andreas, however, had never been introduced to cow pies before (African cows are rather different in this respect). So he thought he would jump on this natural pancake to see what would happen. Maybe it would explode into a cloud of spores like the large fungi do in Africa—he, like his mother, has always been quick to pick up on scientific experiments in ordinary situations. But the object did not explode. It did something worse—it slid. Andreas was quite surprised to find himself on the ground amid the laughter of the onlookers. At this point he realized this was no fungus he had jumped on.

Even when we can correctly identify the flora and fauna, our reactions to nature can still differ from the "average American's" in subtle (and not so subtle) ways. One furlough, as we were taking a walk with my brother Dave in a state park, he suddenly stopped in front of me to look at something on the ground. As I got closer I realized to my horror it was a dreaded snake. I grabbed the kids, shoved them back, and yelled hysterically, "SNAKE! Get back!" My kids obeyed, but my brother remained where he was. I looked at him in amazement and said urgently, "Dave, a snake! Get back!" I nearly added, "Get your machete quick and kill it," but since he had no machete, this would not do much good. He just stood there looking at me like I was crazy and said, "Why should I move? I want to look at the snake." I soon learned that there are no poisonous snakes in that area.

Of course we do not always react in fear to the "wildlife." We were once eating at a friend's house, sitting around the kitchen table and having a lovely meal, when a mouse suddenly shot around the corner of the room. Instantly two people got up and dashed after it: one was the determined husband of the house, and the other was I—an avowed mouse killer. I never stopped to think how people in an American house would react to a guest pulling off her sandal and running with wild abandon after a mouse. This was what we always did in Africa— "all hands on deck." We would not want the little beast to get away, would we? We tried to corner the mouse but it eventually escaped. As I walked defeated back to the table, I noticed the astonished looks directed towards me. Had I come from another planet? Maybe. A planet plentifully stocked with mice that I am continually at war with.

One of the most profound "out of sync" experiences happened to another missionary on furlough. She was at a party when a firecracker exploded nearby. Instantly she dove under a table but found another man was already there. She looked at him sheepishly and said, "What war were you in?"

When I heard this story it reminded me of the time, soon after some political unrest in Ivory Coast, when a string of firecrackers went off near our administrative center in Abidjan. Our reaction at that time was not what you would expect on a typical July day in the States. A group of husbands dashed out of their apartments and started running up to the roof to see if there was gunfire again by the university across the valley. On the way up they were muttering, "Oh, no. Not again." Just before they reached the roof, someone met them and said, "It's okay. It's only fireworks over by the hotel this time."

To you we may appear to be ordinary Americans, but we are not. Our experiences have changed us in many ways. But if you are inclined to look at us askance or laugh at our expense in one of our "out of sync" moments, just wait—we may do the same to you when you visit us in Africa.

50

Goodbyes

The first condition of happiness, reasons Augustine, is that it be permanent. To love what can be lost is to live in fear. Freedom from fear, therefore, can be found only in the immutable possession of an unchanging object and the only object independent of flux is God.

—Gordon H. Clark

Goodbyes are a natural part of life, but in some lines of work they are far too frequent to be comfortable. We belong to a group in constant flux seeing many people come and go. This is the life of a missionary. I rarely cry now at a parting because I have prepared for it as inevitable. It is only afterwards, in a quiet moment, the tears begin to flow at the memory of a friend who has left our lives once again, or of our extended family far away on the other side of the ocean. In missionary life goodbyes are as frequent as greetings, and the special people in your closest sphere are continually changing. When we leave our friends and family across the ocean, God brings in others to replace them for a time, but eventually we lose them too.

Of our dearest friends on the mission field, in our earlier years, was a couple nearing retirement age. They operated the CMA guest house b the ocean. People said the wife and I were like two peas in a pod. She liked to climb trees; so did I. She liked to ride the big waves; so did I. She always wanted to go around the next bend of the trail in the tangled rain forest; so did I. She had an incurable adventuresome spirit; so had I. She was the instigator and I was her accomplice. She had the drive; I gave the encouragement. We worked well together. On one of our more infamous outings she looked over at me and said, "You know, not an awful lot of women would do this with me." We both had another thing very much in common: sedate, sensible and calm husbands who would occasionally worry about us.

This couple was mentor, friend, and family in a place where our old friends and true family were far away. They were ready to retire and left our lives to go to another life back in the States. We knew it would happen but it was still painful. We said our goodbyes rather unemotionally. We acted as if we would see each other next month but we both knew better. Things were going to change.

Though missionaries are a highly mobile community, it is a deep, rich community. Even though its members constantly move on to different assignments, they still have friends all over the world. We have gained from each of our friends in special ways. I learned from my older friend how to accept whatever God gives us in life and carry on. Their departure would be difficult, but as with anything difficult in life, they had accepted it and moved on—now so would we. I knew another couple would be taking their place but I was determined this time not to know them. I was determined not to care, because I knew their mission moved them around often. How could I love someone only to have her taken away again? When they came, I tried for a short time not to care, but soon they too had stolen their way into our hearts.

We had fun together. The wife and I had a tamer relationship than I'd had with my former accomplice, but we still hit it off and they changed our lives. They again became the family that we lacked. I learned much from her, but especially how to bear up under severe trial and see beauty and God's grace through the hardest circumstances. She lived out a beautiful faith that grew and developed slowly through years of sickness and chronic fatigue.

Then came the day that I again dreaded. They were called to move on to another field, and I felt that old familiar ache inside. When they came to say goodbye, I felt numb. I wanted to cry but I couldn't. I knew I would cry later—I always did when someone I loved was taken away from me, which was often. I tried to think that this time would be different. It never was and we both knew it. Another close friend was moving on in ministry and out of my immediate life, and I would miss her.

Once I was sitting by a missionary collegue during a conference, and she commented about this difficult aspect of missionary life. She said there are only two options for survival: to love quickly and deeply, or not to love at all. In the former course you hurt badly every time you move on and a relationship is broken, but in the latter you shut yourself off from loving anyone, and while it is true that you do not hurt when someone leaves, you also begin slowly to die within—no one can live without giving and receiving love.

We have a common bond with other missionaries and we need each other more in a place where life is rough and comforts are few. Background, interests, and age no longer seem to matter much. Our friendships tend to run deep and fast making them all the more difficult to break off. How can you face the subtle prolonged grief of always saying goodbye? When you love deeply it rips you apart and leaves you hurting. Some people cannot face it and leave to put down more permanent roots back home. I cannot blame them. Though we repeatedly hurt, we also repeatedly run to the Lord who heals all our wounds. We cry and He comforts us. We grieve and He holds us. The more we hurt the more He heals us, and the more it becomes apparent that there is no end to the fountain of His grace.

As I stood in our no-frills kitchen in the village with the evening breeze coming through our open window and the night quickly following with the setting sun, I felt the tears welling up inside me as I remembered once again those who had left. Yet God was there. He would always be. He is the one thing that never changes. He only is always sure to fill that emptiness completely. This life is only temporary; we are just passing through and moving on to better ground. We are doing our best with what we have, trying to please our Lord, until we arrive safely home to our final resting place. There we shall see all those we have been parted from for so long, and we will greet them—never to say "goodbye" again.

51

Entering the Door

I gave birth to our two youngest children in a Baptist hospital located two days' drive to the north. We were well situated there in a guesthouse on the hospital compound. Of these two births in Africa, one was very easy and one was very difficult. It was not difficult because it was a complicated birth; it was just very long and painful. I don't know why some births must be difficult and some easy, but I know I learned an awful lot from the difficult labor. For the first time I thought I could actually visualize what death might be like.

It was night and Csaba and I walked in the darkness by the doctors' houses to pass the painful moments of labor. The night was silent and still compared to a busy day at the bustling hospital. We could see the stars beyond the mango trees, stars that sang out hope through the dim boughs of the trees obscuring them. I was hurting so badly I could barely enjoy the stroll or the beautiful night. Our walking came in stops and starts, my breathing was difficult, and my body was tired. The night wore on until we inched our way to the hospital for the last agonizing stretch. I asked the doctor if he had ever known anyone to have a labor as difficult as this. He looked up at me with sympathy and said, "Yes, my wife. Hers was pretty bad, but she made it just fine. Hang in there."

I asked him if he ever gave pain medication to those who wanted it. He said pain medication was in short supply at the mission hospital and reserved only for true emergencies (which I was not). I just wanted it to end. During times like this it was easy to forget a baby was coming and there was a purpose for the pain.

In the night air and in the small hours of the morning, I thought how giving birth was a bit like dying. I had to pass through a door of agony, a kind of death, to get the gift of the child—a gift of life. When at last I gave birth that morning, the pain and discomfort left instantly and I seemed to enter a new world. Morning had dawned: how different from the darkness, how like another world that day was!

Death really is a birth, an open door to life. On one side of the door is sickness and pain, a long confinement to a room you will not leave again. There are worried faces around the bed, silence and a darkness settles before the dawn of morning. The people left on this side of the door cannot see what really happens at the end of the story in the unseen realm beyond the door. I can only imagine what it is like when God takes the hand of His child near death and leads him, comforting him, knowing well the intense joy to come. It will only be a moment—just a moment longer. Then the beloved one slips away through the door of death and leaves the rest behind in their grief. They are not yet allowed to enter. And what of that one who has just left? In an instant, he is plunged through the door and into the paradise on the other side. In an instant all pain has vanished, night has become day, crying has ceased and turned into songs of joy. In a moment everything changes, and Jesus wipes away the tears, holding His child close, welcoming him home.

The only thing to fear about death is to meet it not having truly known the Lord, not having bowed down to Him as Master, not having received the gift of His Son and having believed in His word. Then death is truly an ominous thing with no loving face to meet us on the other end. Instead of plunging into light, we would be plunged into an ever-deepening darkness from which all hope would vanish. Rejecting Jesus in this life means we have rejected the comfort we could have had, the hand that would have lovingly led us through that door into all eternity.

Rejoicing, praising, and an eternity of joy wait for those who enter into the laughing side of that world. At last they are with the One who so lovingly led them through their mortal lives, comforted them through pain, and took their hand through death. It all happens when, in a twinkling of triumph, their Savior releases them into peace and happiness that will never end. It all comes by entering that door. Those of us left behind see only the empty room and the empty bed. We feel the loneliness and pain of separation. We see only the blank face of this side of the door. We can hope and trust in faith for what will come, because God has said what will come in His word and He is faithful. "And Jesus said to him, 'Assuredly, I say to you, today you will be with me in Paradise'" (Luke 23:43).

Part VIII
School

Home schooling in the village has been both fun and challenging. One of our challenges is the limited resources we have to work with. The fun comes in all the unique opportunities we have living in the tropical environment of Africa. God provides in one way or another and the benefits of our village experience have far out-weighed the detriments. Here is a look into some of our more memorable homeschooling experiences. Most of them occurred when the children were all of elementary school age.

52

Unusual Art

It was art day and we were in between shopping trips with no decent paper to use for painting. The next trip was not scheduled for some time, so we had to think of something else to use. Someone thought of the old white rooster. Sure, why not? He would make great "paper" for a watercolor project. Certainly he would not mind. The old white cock was duly procured, and the watercolor artists set to work to transform him into something more exciting. The cock was very tame and stood there quite docilely as the kids had fun dotting and striping him with all the colors of the rainbow. He soon became what you might call a modern art chicken. The kids laughed and giggled as they watched "His Highness" change into something new and grand. The cock really did not need any more boosting of his self-image as he was already the king of the yard.

Once the art project was done, we let the king go. He pranced off happily with his new look to survey his kingdom. Suddenly something blindsided him with incredible force. The king wheeled around and stood face to face with a lesser cock whose head was down and neck feathers out in a serious challenge. This usurper was a king hopeful who was supposed to know he was only a cock errant. The multi-colored king looked at this two-bit nobody and wondered how such a despicable creature had the nerve to challenge him. In fact, the lesser cock challenged him because he did not recognize the white cock anymore. He thought a new cock had entered the king's realm and as cock errant he was going to fight him to keep his position. There is nothing more humiliating than being bumped down lower than you already are by a newcomer—it would just take that much longer to make it to the top.

A cockfight ensued and the lesser cock did not back down until the force of the king had got the better of him and he ran away in submission, tail down and chest held low, still chased by the king, who had the difficult task of running at high speed while still maintaining his dignity. If you are a dominant cock, social etiquette dictates you must run in a certain way, prancing with head high and chest out, or the ladies will not be impressed. It is not easy to run this way at an all-out pace but the king made an effort, and the dispute between the two cocks soon ended.

After all the fun that morning, we decided that during next week's art and science day we would see what else could be done to mess up the pecking order. The next week we took the lesser cock and painted him in the same fashion we had the king. When we set him down in the chicken yard, the king did not attack him even though he did not recognize him. We pondered over this unexpected outcome and became doubly confused when the other cocks under him came forth to challenge him. Why did the dominant rooster not see this "newcomer" as a threat? Someone suggested wattle length had something to do with it. Maybe if a cock has small wattles he is not considered much to fight with—could wattle length be an indicator in chicken society of whether you are a "man" or not?

We made some fake wattles out of red felt and attached them with a piece of pipe cleaner around the lesser cock's neck. If our theory was correct, this would boost his position and the dominant cock would again be aroused to wrath. We let the lesser cock out in the yard with his fake wattles, and sure enough the king was threatened. He made a terrific prancing dash for this young usurper but this time there was no fight. Cock number two made a fast submissive dash for the nearest bush, false wattles flapping gaily in the breeze. We were thrilled. What else could we do with this new bit of information?

We took a hen and put the fake wattles on her to see if we could confuse the king. Would the king mistake her for a cock? If he lunged for her, we could always scare him away before the poor hen was too scandalized. She, in the meantime, was clueless that she was now 'a cock' and went happily back to eating grain on the ground. The result was interesting. The king came over on the double to inspect this new crea-ture, which looked threatening since it had the telltale red flags of a fighter, but it was not acting like it should. I watched the king inspect the hen, who was oblivious to everything and quite content to keep eating. The king eyed her suspiciously, not sure how to respond. I could just see him sizing her up in his mind. "Hmmmm . . . this looks like a hen. It acts like a hen. It even sounds like a hen, but it has the badge of a cock around its neck. This does not make sense." Finally, in the end, the cock made a display of dominance by drooping his wings and circling around her a few times. He then trotted contentedly away. Whatever he, she, or it was, he was now dominant over it and the problem was solved.

Our village chickens have provided us with many things: art projects glorified, science projects pondered over, and pets that are loved—inter-esting creatures of God's world that give us delight.

53

Obstacle Course

We have our own personal cross-country course on our property. Hans calls it an *obstacle* course, which is actually much closer to the reality. I decided to set up a path around our property after experiencing exercise on the public soccer field in our village. Inevitably, as the kids started running around the soccer field, we would collect a variety of passers-by who would stand around and gawk at them. It never failed. When the kids would take off for their first lap, the boys in their shorts and Noai in her skirt, a group of market women would pass by. One by one they would put their loads down on the ground and then, congregating in little groups, would comment on the spectacle in their soft tonal language. Occasionally they would giggle and point. Then another group of ladies would come and do the same. By the time the kids were halfway around the field, we would have collected quite a crowd. Nobody seemed to be in a hurry to go anywhere when they could stop and watch such a grand sight as my kids doing laps around the field. I am not sure what they thought. Maybe they were wondering what the kids were running from, or maybe they thought Noai was angry and chasing the boys. I knew the boys had a loathing for giggling market women and so this afternoon spectacle would have to stop.

So I made a private course around our property instead. It is really a very interesting course. I did not design it like that, but under the circumstances we had little else to work with. The children start off from the front yard and head toward our cocoa forest, a dark, low group of trees with yellow cocoa pods hanging from the trunks. (Csaba had me sweep away the leaves from underneath the trees to keep the kids from surprising vipers unaware.) After passing through this dark section, they come out in the sunshine and run on a thick carpet of grass sprinkled with pineapples. Then they pass through a green tunnel leading into an area of heavy bush—what I call the "back forty." As you run through it, it is like running under a low, vaulted ceiling of green with scattered light coming through and sprinkling down on the path below. Someone always goes in beforehand to make sure all the green mambas are scared away—they tend to look like the bushes and do not take kindly to being disturbed.

When the kids come out of the tunnel they go past the pond and hear the multiple plops of panicked frogs jumping into the safety of the water. Next they head up behind the office where the course diverges: the walkers (Csaba and I) go one way, while the runners go another. The runners go up the hill through the chicken yard dodging hysterical hens. Our old dog is often awakened by the thundering crew and sometimes joins them as they pass by. Originally I wanted the runners to take the other course behind the chicken pen, but after much thought I decided it was not wise. The way is longer and goes past Csaba's African killer-bee hives. These bees tend to be agitated by fast movements, and running with a cloud of bees behind you, though probably motivating, is not very fun, I decided to divert the kids through the chicken yard.

So while the runners are thundering up towards the front with the dog following on their heels, Csaba and I are walking softly past the beehives, turning a corner and slipping by the old stump where we think the elusive cobra lives. After this we duck under the bougainvillea hedge and enter the chicken yard where we re-fluster the hens and are joined by the dog as we head up around the house. This will be repeated for five or six laps. It is great fun and sure beats enduring the giggling market ladies. And no—Noai is not chasing the boys.

54

The Guineas and Their Mama

It was Wednesday, our science day, and I laid out a project for the kids to do: based on their knowledge of animal behavior, they were to correct a slight barnyard problem we had. One of our hens had successfully hatched seven guinea fowl, which naturally followed her everywhere as chicks normally do. This was fine until we realized our guinea fowl had no intention of ever leaving their "mama." I now had seven fully-grown guinea fowl who thought they were still chicks. This problem would definitely put a damper on future batches of chicks for this hen, so my children's task was to try to get the guinea fowl to loathe their mother.

The idea was simple. All we had to do was to alter her appearance so they would be frightened by her and leave her. Since chickens are of little brain, we felt the initial scare would bring them to their senses. From previous experiments we learned that chickens largely recognize each other by sight, so the kids tried to change the hen's appearance by attaching a paper jacket around her body and adding paper streamers on the back to look like a cock's tail. She did not seem to mind the alteration since she was a very tame hen, and she looked so different it was sure to work.

We took her outside and set her down on the ground by her guineas to see how they would react, but a most unexpected thing happened. As soon as she touched the ground she gave a loud squawk and took off at a run. In her flight she somehow managed to trip over her tails and did a few barrel rolls before dashing off toward the rabbit cage at full speed.

Her guineas were terrified at this apparition and huddled in a close circle, jabbering like seven machine guns.

The hen ran madly, as if she were being chased by a dozen weasels. This was actually not too far from the truth—we had not counted on the streamers flapping in the wind behind her, simulating the appearance of many weasels on her tail. She dashed for safety towards a group of hens nervously begackling at the spectacle, and the whole flock exploded in all directions. They flew for shelter, wailing loudly as if they were all going to die. By now the king came onto the scene, ready to defend his kingdom from all ills. He dashed off after his ill-fated wife, crowing that he would save her. When she saw the cock running in the same direction, away from the supposed weasels, this confirmed her worst fears and she shrieked again telling everyone to take cover.

The barnyard was now in an uproar with the guineas jabbering, the chickens cackling, the hen shrieking, the rooster wailing, and the dog barking. It only stopped when the hen dove into a bush. We walked over, extracted her, and took off her coat and streamers. This certainly was not what we had expected. The guineas were supposed to be terrified, not the hen herself and the whole rest of the menagerie. We let her loose and immediately she was surrounded again by her entourage of guinea fowl, all chirring terms of endearment to her. She in turn told them about her gallant near escape from the dreaded weasels.

One project had failed, but at least all was calm again. We would be back to the drawing board for the next week.

55

God is Good

The sun was setting and I was sitting with some of the children in the wheelbarrow on a bag of corn mash. We were all silently looking up at the sky. My young son spoke up, breaking my reverie, "You know, Mama, it's another happy day. All our days are happy here."

"Yes, they are." I replied. "God has been very good to us."

We continued to watch the huge clouds loll lazily over the shadowy hills as the sun slipped behind the treetops. The chickens were contentedly making bedtime noises in their appointed spots in the trees, while the only other noise that could be heard was an occasional "Good morning bird" from the parrot. Yes, life was good—so good.

Epilogue: The Work

WHAT WE DO

We work under the auspices of the Wycliffe Bible Translators, who seek to assist the Church in making disciples of all nations through Bible translation. Aspects of the task include surveying languages (determining whether they need a translation), analyzing the sound system and developing an alphabet if one doesn't exist, preparing pedagogical materials, teambuilding, literacy training (including teacher training), publishing, and finally, translating the Scriptures. Our goal is to provide God's word to every person who needs it, a goal which results in changed lives, maturing believers, and growing, self-sustaining churches.

TEAMBUILDING

The first step in building a translation team is to find the right translator. Before we even arrived in Bakwéland, Csaba had prayed a long time about this. He had first worked with an older man but found this was not the best solution since in Africa one cannot tell an older man what to do and when to do it. He started looking for a younger man who would respect his authority and be of good character. He found Alexis, a young man who had been partially educated in the local French school but had never traveled outside of Bakwéland. (Not many Bakwé fully understand French.) More importantly, Alexis was from the other side of the village, which had felt snubbed when we built our house on the opposite side. When we accepted him, they finally accepted us.

Alexis helped Csaba learn the language and the culture but announced one day he was not a Christian. Csaba replied that it was okay and he could still work for us. Alexis said he desired to read the Bible in French to find out what was in it. Csaba told him to go ahead but to be careful because God would hold him accountable for what he would learn. After reading some and knowing he would be held accountable for that knowledge, he quickly shut the Bible and put it away. He was profoundly disturbed. But the next day he was drawn again to God's word. This time he read on and on and somewhere along the way God opened his heart and he surrendered his life to Christ. Csaba talked to him about it and taught him from the Bible. With this new life in Christ, he now had a purpose and a reason for being on the translation team. He was eager to help translate this wonderful word into his own language for his people.

PROGRESSION OF THE WORK

Csaba spent much of his time first building the team. After Alexis, Csaba hired and trained Perez and then Firmin. Csaba had a vision of making the team into a functioning body that could one day run on its own. How does one take three men with little training and experience with the outside world and turn them into a self-sufficient team? Csaba did it very slowly and carefully. His goal was to teach them everything that he knew, step by step, and when they were ready he would turn it over to them.

In an African society the younger folk learn from their elders mainly by watching. The elders take them wherever they go and they work side by side together. The child is always there, watching and taking part in all aspects of life. It is a mentored way of learning rather than a classroom situation where a teacher talks constantly but remains totally separate from the students. Csaba wanted to follow this same mentoring method, so in everything he did Alexis was there, watching and learning. He watched as Csaba explained how to use the computer, how to run certain programs, and later how to fix the computer. He learned about finances and how to organize them on the computer. He learned how to deal with the other missionaries who helped with the project in various ways. Most of all, he learned how to live the Christian life as he watched Csaba in action in various situations. When an interesting problem would arise, they would often have long conversations together about to how to handle it.

One strategy very effective in the past was fellowshipping over a meal. Csaba and the team in the earlier years would eat breakfast together and talk about their day. In the conversation, Csaba would share with them his vision of where they were going and how to get there, for a vision is not taught, it is caught. And slowly they were catching it.

With this increasing knowledge came greater and greater responsibility. The men formed the PTAB (*Projet de Traduction et d'Alphabetisation en langue Bakwé* or "The Bakwé Translation and Literacy Project") and appointed a president, treasurer, and literacy and public relations manager. They learned their roles. They printed literature and sold it. They learned how to budget resources and take the profits from the sales to use towards printing more books. They got involved in a money-making side business renting out chairs, the profits of which would be used to supplement the literacy budget. They also had another side business in desktop publishing, the proceeds of which went towards paying the salary of a secretary.

The team was an integral part in the decision-making process for the direction of the project. Their opinions mattered. Their advice was heeded. Their projects were installed. Csaba had meetings with them every Friday and would again seek to impart the vision of what they were trying to do overall. Then they would make immediate goals in line with their vision. Sometimes they wanted to go in a direction Csaba was hesitant about. He knew there would be problems with a particular course, but if they were adamant, and it wasn't dangerous to the project, he would let them go ahead. This way they could see the results of their actions, and in a failed venture could learn from their mistakes. It was all part of learning. One has to be free to fail, free to learn and grow through the process. They had come to the point where they felt like they owned the ministry and were willing to give of their own time and money to help out.

Our goal is to build leaders who will function on their own and move on to help other teams as well. We see them in the future using their skills, consulting others, and knowing how to support themselves when we are gone. We have been greatly encouraged by them. They once wrote Csaba a letter saying how grateful they were to him for opening up his life to them, and how they appreciated the influence he has had on their lives. This letter was followed by a gift of money.

WORKSHOPS

Part of our work is to continue our own training in areas where we ourselves need more help. We often travel five hours north to our workshop center in Bouaké to attend workshops on literacy, translation, grammar, phonology, discourse analysis, lexicology, and many other areas relating to our work. Sometimes Csaba's Bakwé team is required to come along too. One time at a literacy workshop, the team was in the dining area late at night trying to put together a story for a beginning literacy primer using only a small number of key words. This was difficult. The story they put together was so ridiculous. When I walked into the cafeteria that night, to find out when I would ever see Csaba again, I found them all nearly doubled on the floor in laughter. They were holding their sides and laughing so hard (Csaba included) that no one could talk to me for a whole minute. I had no idea what had happened. Csaba mentioned, when he could catch his breath, the story was so funny with the words they used that—I guess you just had to be there.

PROBLEMS

With our team's increasing responsibility in areas new to them, there were some rather predictable problems. They often messed up the computer in learning to run it. The accounting books were sometimes in disarray. Many times Csaba would spend hours trying to unravel the incredible mess made of the finances when someone failed to enter costs in the right categories. The chair rental business almost collapsed when money was borrowed from it to keep the literacy accounts afloat. Fixing it took time, time to unravel, time to teach, time to give, time to help them learn and try again. Putting responsibility into their hands slowed us down a little, but well worth it—we are in the process of making leaders.

Csaba learned a great deal about how to manage a team. Some of the most important things he needed to know to make the ministry work were never taught in school. He learned to be patient in trying times, to believe the best about a person instead of automatically assuming the worst. He learned not to accuse someone of a fault until he knows the full story, told in a calm and unthreatening environment. He learned to always look to the past to see just how far these men have already come instead of being discouraged at how far they still have to go. He learned to be firm and to have high expectations, but also to give encouragement when the load seemed too much to bear. Most of all he learned not to give up on anyone when they failed. Even though the full force of consequences must sometimes be felt, he teaches them how to succeed and he will be right alongside them to try it again.

In his time spent counseling them in their problems, helping them in their crises, teaching them what he knows and being available to them, he has gained their respect and loyalty. It is a loyalty that will motivate them to continue to work for their leader even when the will to do so in a normal situation would have failed long before. That loyalty has been the backbone of our team.

WE'VE ONLY JUST BEGUN

Our work has only just begun. There is still years' worth of work to make the men in the team the leaders they need to be to run the ministry entirely by themselves. All of this takes time: time to counsel, to fellowship over a meal, to take part in their lives, to teach all aspects of the work, and to open up God's word to them; it is an all-inclusive training. Making leaders does take time, but in doing so it shows just how much we care.

In the meantime the translation and literacy work goes on slowly. Our ultimate goal is to help the Church at large by providing Scriptures for the Bakwé people. One time Csaba asked questions in French to an African man about a passage in Scripture to check the man's level of understanding. His answers showed he had come up with an opposite meaning from what the text truly stated. Csaba then read the text in the man's native tongue and he understood it for the first time. Having the Word available to everyone is the backbone of a thriving local church. If we did not believe this we would not be doing this work. It is this vision that keeps us going.

Our desire is to create, with the help of men who will be leaders and examples in the society, a quality translation to last for many years. Due to the influence of God's word preached and lived out by these leaders we desire to see churches established, culture changed, and society redeemed.

It only takes a few good men to start the process of change. We are looking many years past our own lifetime. We think about a time when the knowledge of the Lord will cover the earth like the waters cover the sea. And, in the great scheme of things, when we are long gone, when the years fade away and are engulfed into the past, a people who were once small on this earth will become great in the eyes of the Lord.

Appendix

The sketches in this book are true to what actually happened to the best of my memory, except in a few cases where to set a scene and help people understand culture or place, I combined two separate experiences to achieve the full effect. I did this in "The Revenge of the Market Ladies," "A Sketch on Death," and a "Trip to Town."

THE CAST OF CHARACTERS

We are members of Wycliffe Bible Translators of the Ivory Coast-Mali branch and work in a little village in the west of Ivory Coast. There are six people in our family. My husband's name is Csaba, which is quite the mouthful when you run across it for the first time. It is a Hungarian name (his father is from Hungary). The computer always gives us trouble at the spell check and asks us if we want to change his name to "Scab." We do not. Csaba is leader of the Bakwé project, as well as my personal counselor and general hysteria calmer. The honorable sons are Hans (age 15), an amateur scientist and specialist in booby traps for unsuspecting younger brothers; Andreas (11), a grapefruit hunter and archeologist of old pig pens; and Jeremiah (8), who holds first place in the "Holding on to a Tree Limb for Dear Life" competition. Our only daughter Noai (13) is an animal lover and enthusiast who raises orphaned wildlife (this includes her "Adopt an Abandoned Chick from Thoughtless Hen" program) and trains indignant cats.

The children are blond-haired variations of a single theme—Csaba. (Only I stand out with my reddish hair.) At the time of this writing we have been in the village for 14 years, and the span of most of these writings covers a period of two years. The approximate ages of the children at the time I wrote most of the sketches are fifteen for Hans, eleven for Noai, nine for Andreas, and six for Jeremiah. If the ages are younger than that range, I indicated their ages in the text.

The Bakwé team consists of three men. Yepi Alexis (translator) is on the quiet side, yet bold. Apart from his main job of translation, he is Csaba's right hand man. Gnagbe Firmin (literacy specialist) has a heart for evangelism and is a great asset to the team. Kle Perez (literacy specialist) leads the literacy projects and the Bakwé newspaper. He directs the Harrist church choir and is a gifted writer.

Of our household help, Javier (the cook) stands out. Originally from Burkina Faso, he is a hard worker, has a great exuberance for life, and is a great help to us. A number of people have filled our other position (yard work and laundry) and then moved on. Currently it is Moïse, who is also a hard worker and very respectful.

THE HARRIST CHURCH

The Harrist Church was founded by William Wade Harris, a Liberian man who preached along the coast of West Africa between 1913 and 1915. Harris preached a simple gospel, burned fetishes (charms), and baptized his converts. During his eighteen-month evangelistic tour in Côte d'Ivoire, Harris had an extraordinary following of one to two hundred thousand converts. Unfortunately not much is known about the content of the gospel he preached, except that he taught the basic tenets of the Christian faith: worship of the one true God, worship on the Lord's Day, the Ten Commandments, and above all, a great respect for the Bible as the word of God. Wherever Harris went he told his converts to wait for the white man who would bring them the Bible and not to listen to any white man who came without it. He also told his converts to send their children to schools so they could learn to read the Bible. The Bakwé did not receive the Harrist teaching until 1966 when a delegation from a Harrist faction came into the area and converted the entire people group. Since then the Bakwé Harrists have been slowly brought under the main Harris denomination, and many syncretistic practices are being corrected in light of the Scriptures.